Pelican Books
The Politics of Mental Handicap

Frank Thomas was born in 1947 at Bethnal Green. In 1972 he began a course on the education of mentally handicapped children as a result of a one-off visit to an adult training centre. After prematurely finishing this course, through disillusion with the education system, he became a nursing assistant in a large subnormality hospital. During his six months there he kept a diary of his experience, which he states was 'a means of preserving my sanity in such a place'. Since writing this book, Frank Thomas has worked with homeless families, as a volunteer in a large psychiatric hospital, as an instructor in a work centre for the disabled, and as an assistant warden in a hostel for ex-psychiatric patients. He is also writing a play about a children's home and is working on several other projects.

He is married and lives with his wife in Blackburn, Lancashire.

Joanna Ryan was born in 1942 and was educated at Oxford High School and New Hall, Cambridge, where she obtained a Ph.D. in psychology in 1967. She then did research at the Unit for Medical Applications of Psychology in Cambridge, on the development of mentally handicapped children, and also on the beginnings of speech in babies. In 1970 she was made the first woman fellow of King's College, Cambridge. She moved to London in 1974 and became involved in community and feminist politics, and in self-help therapy. Since 1977 she has worked as a therapist and counsellor, mainly at Battersea Action and Counselling Centre until this was closed. She then worked on a mental patients' rights project at Camden Community Law Centre, and recently has worked as research officer at MIND. She is expecting her first child.

The Politics of Mental Handicap

Joanna Ryan
with
Frank Thomas

Penguin Books

Penguin Books Ltd, Harmondsworth, Middlesex, England
Penguin Books, 625 Madison Avenue, New York, New York 10022, U.S.A.
Penguin Books Australia Ltd, Ringwood, Victoria, Australia
Penguin Books Canada Ltd, 2801 John Street, Markham, Ontario,
Canada L3R 1B4
Penguin Books (N.Z.) Ltd, 182–190 Wairau Road, Auckland 10,
New Zealand

First published 1980

Copyright © Joanna Ryan and Frank Thomas, 1980
All rights reserved

Made and printed in Great Britain by
Richard Clay (The Chaucer Press) Ltd
Bungay, Suffolk
Set in Monotype Times

For Jacob

Contents

Preface

After half a century of silence, we have seen recently an unprecedented level of public inquiry into the lives of mentally handicapped people. Most of this has focused on the mental subnormality hospitals in which many handicapped people live. These hospitals have been in a state of crisis for the last ten years: for the first time, the lives of their inmates have been brought out into the open, to confront the society that could do nothing but put them away.

Our book is both a product of this crisis, and a reflection upon it. It contains a diary and a commentary, each written from the standpoint of our own experience. Frank Thomas worked as a nursing assistant and volunteer in various hospitals and schools; I was a research worker in a university department, visiting these places in order to study the development of mentally handicapped children. Frank's diary records the daily experience of life on the ward, the realities of those who live and work there; my commentary provides a historical and theoretical perspective on this. Each amplifies the other.

Frank wrote his diary without any thought of publication, as a stream of incidents and observations, mostly unconnected to one another. It was a means of expressing how he felt, an attempt to grasp the situation he and the patients were in. As he originally wrote it, there was little sense of development over time; a reflection, perhaps, of the static nature of ward life. I have selected and edited about half of the original diary, and changed the order of separate passages, so that the diary is no longer chronological to read, but arranged around particular topics and events. This makes for easier reading, but may mask the fragmentation of daily life.

The identities of the patients, the staff, the various wards and the actual hospital have all been concealed by a complete change of names: any resemblance to people or wards in existing hospitals is entirely accidental.

The rest of the book is an attempt to understand why we as a society have treated mentally handicapped people so badly, and why they are still so stigmatized, the source of so much despair to themselves and others. I have tried to analyse why it is that the spirit of reform, that stretches back nearly 150 years, has been so frequently frustrated and undermined – an issue that is particularly important with so much promised reform in the air. By taking the relationships between patients and staff in the hospital as a microcosm of the wider reality, a crystallization of our social history, I have tried to disentangle the historical, institutional and personal forces that all too often lead to the dehumanization of 'them'. It has to be said, because it is so often anticipated, that this book is not intended as a vendetta against the ward staff, but is rather an attempt to show how the realities of ward life are the end result of a complex social process that we all participate in. The hospitals are the last point in a system of exclusion and disposal, the staff the guardians of our deepest fears and prejudices.

Chapter 1, by way of introduction, discusses how the social category of mentally handicapped people is created, and why it is that the medical profession has so much control over their lives, when it is so inappropriate to most of their needs. Readers who find this chapter too abstract may want to turn first to Chapter 2, which contains the bulk of Frank's diary, depicting many aspects of ward life. In Chapter 3, using more of Frank's diary and also other contemporary studies, I go deeper into the question of what determines the nature of staff–patient relationships within the hospital. Chapter 4, using similar material, brings in the 'normal' world outside the hospital, examining how other people relate to the patients. Chapter 5 is a historical discussion, which tries to show how the situation of the previous chapters can have arisen. It looks particularly at the changing definitions and concepts of mentally handicapped people, as these relate to the practice of their containment and treatment. It also shows how proposed reforms in the way society deals with them have almost always been tied to the possibility of some improvement in their abilities and behaviour, as a condition of greater acceptance. Chapter 6 brings this theme into the present, with a look at modern ideologies of behavioural change and 'normalization', within the context of our present hospitals. Chapter 7 examines the resistance of the medical and nursing professions to proposed reforms, and concludes by suggesting what it is that staff, and other people in close daily contact with severely handicapped people, need in order not to have to adopt attitudes that lead to the eventual rejection of their charges as inexorably 'different'.

This has not been an easy book to write and for the same reasons may not be altogether easy to read. I have had to meet my own resistances to the subject matter, to steer a path between my own despair and my inclination to withdraw to a safer distance, to forget the unacceptable. It is no part of my intention to hold the reader's interest through guilt. Rather, my hope is that this book will enable readers to look at their own reactions to mentally handicapped people more clearly; and to assess the various proposals about what should be done 'for' or 'about' mentally handicapped people in the light of these. By providing a wider perspective than simply that of the provision of services, I hope that this book will contribute to the current debates about the lives of mentally handicapped people and those connected with them.

J.R.

Acknowledgements

Many people have contributed directly or indirectly to the writing of this book. I would particularly like to thank the members of the Medical Psychology Unit, Cambridge, for encouraging me through years of somewhat isolated research, as I gradually dropped the encumbrances of academic psychology, and saw the social reality of those I was meant to be studying; and Liz Cooper for hastening this process and making me look at how others, including myself, behaved towards mentally handicapped people. Numerous friends in the Women's Movement, Big Flame and Red Therapy contributed towards a perspective where the political does not exclude the personal, and where action in the present is informed by a self-conscious and critical knowledge of the past. I have greatly appreciated Julia Vellacott's encouragement and editorial advice, and I would like to thank Suzanne Puddefoot for some helpful sub-editing. I am especially grateful to Lucy Goodison, Paul Morrison, Susie Orbach, Ann Scott, and Sheila Young for their unstinting support and encouragement; and I would like to thank David Ingleby and Martin Richards for invaluable last-minute inspiration.

I am grateful for permission to quote from the following: Campaign for the Mentally Handicapped, various publications; R. Edgerton, *The Cloak of Competence* (University of California Press); P. Nichols, *A Day in the Death of Joe Egg* (Faber & Faber) and A. Shearer and R. Kugel, *Changing Patterns of Residential Services for the Mentally Handicapped*.

Chapter 1

Definitions of Difference

There are nearly 50,000 people who live in mental handicap hospitals in Britain. The majority have been there for more than five years, many for more than twenty.[1] The hospitals themselves are part of the National Health Service; some contain as many as 1,500 people.[2] The buildings are often old and huge, the grounds spacious.

What people in these hospitals supposedly have in common is that they are 'mentally handicapped'. Such people have been called by many names. The older terms, 'fool' and 'idiot', have passed into ordinary language as common terms of abuse. Names supplant each other very fast in this field, in the illusory search for a designation that is neutral or euphemistic, for example, the American 'exceptional child', or the English 'developmentally young'. It now seems more offensive to call someone 'mentally deficient' (the early twentieth-century term), or 'subnormal' (the mid-twentieth-century term), rather than 'handicapped' (the contemporary term); but the reality for the person concerned may not be so different.

The name 'mentally handicapped' will be used here, except where it is historically inappropriate. It is used with a sense of awkwardness. Many of those defined by it would, and do, reject such a label. 'I'm not handicapped – I can do things', is how one resident of a hospital expressed his protest against this definition of himself.[3]

Many mentally handicapped people are acutely aware of how others see them, of the names they get called:

I've been told I've got no brains where I live – how do you think I felt? Very sarcastic some of them. There's a limit to tease anyone but some of them go too far, beyond the deep end, as they say. I wouldn't mind it occasionally, but they do it too often, crack a joke. That's not fair, is it?[4]

Many of them engage in a constant struggle to seem as much like others as possible:

I don't see why people don't treat me as a normal person instead of some kind of – well, you know, some kind of crazy person. I try so hard to act like a normal person. I never tell people I've been in that . . . institution, and I always treat other people right. I talk right and I act right. I just can't seem to make people treat me like a normal person. Is it because I don't look normal?[5]

Their efforts to appear as ordinary as possible are not helped by the use of clearly stigmatizing labels. It is hardly surprising that many of them refuse to describe themselves in such terms.

'Mental handicap' is also used of extremely different conditions. This is also a source of much pain to those concerned. Mentally handicapped people often find it very hard to differentiate themselves as individuals in the eyes of others, to escape from other people's stereotypes of them. Living in hospital, and being the objects of scientific study, rob them even further of their individuality:

Being in the institution was bad. I got tied up and locked up. I didn't have any clothes of my own, and no privacy. We got beat at times but that wasn't the worst. The real pain came from always being a group. I was never a person. I was part of a group to eat, sleep and everything. As a kid I couldn't figure out who I was. I was part of a group. It was sad.[6]

Frank's diary sharply underlines this point: the patients are frequently seen as 'this lot' or 'those sort of people'. He by contrast tries 'to see a person for what he is, not as one of "them" '.

But, while we may respond to the truth and humanity of this, we cannot leave the question of definition there. Whatever we may feel about the injustice and pain involved, mentally handicapped people confront us with human difference in the starkest way: 'An idiot is someone who knows nothing, can do nothing, wants nothing, and each idiot approaches more or less to this point of incapacity.'[7] Thus wrote Seguin, the nineteenth century's most inspired advocate of special education for idiots. Yet anyone in close contact with such extremely handicapped people (the 'vegetable' or 'cot-and-chair' cases as they are called in hospital) in fact learns the barely perceptible ways in which they express their preferences, their reactions to events around them. They may take food more willingly from one nurse rather than another; they may blink at an unfamiliar sound or smell. What Seguin's description does convey is the effect that these people have on the rest of us: the sense of nothingness they evoke. Seguin indeed called them 'children of the *néant*'.[8] They represent such an extreme of life that we wonder whether they are human at all, in any way like us. Our interaction with them seems so minimal, we wonder what the point of their existence is. Unless we perform specific care-taking tasks for them – feed, wash, change or move them – we do not know who we are for them or who they are for us. Is there any mutual identity we can establish, any reciprocity between us, and if there is, do we want to know about it?

The majority of mentally handicapped people do not approach such extremes, and they themselves would repudiate such an association. For many, part of the distress and stigma of being in hospital is being mixed up with people they see as 'cripples' and 'crazies'.[9] Even so they also confront us with their difference, and with our sense of their difference.

The changing definitions of difference constitute the history of mentally handicapped people. These definitions have always been conceived of by others, never are they the expression of a group of people finding their own identity, their own history. The assertion of difference between people is seldom neutral; it almost always implies some kind of social distance or distinction. The differences between mentally handicapped people and others have mostly been seen negatively, making them a problem to themselves and to others. Only in a few instances has the 'otherness' of mentally handicapped people been valued positively or respected.*

* See Chapters 5 and 7.

This question of difference has been central to those who have tried over the last 150 years to improve the way in which society treats mentally handicapped people. Reformers, at all times, tend to argue that mentally handicapped people are not so different from other people as is thought, that they should not be treated so differently, but should be given at least some of the rights and opportunities that others have. Such arguments nevertheless do not neglect the special needs that handicapped people have and which must be catered for if the differences between them and other people are to be minimized.

There are those on the other hand who emphasize the differences and who argue for a more segregated life for the mentally handicapped. They see the goal of reducing the differences between the handicapped and the rest of society as either impossible, because their potential is allegedly so limited, or simply as undesirable. Both sides of this argument – the optimists and the pessimists as they are sometimes called – do however share the same assumption: that the problem consists in the nature of mentally handicapped people themselves. Their only real argument is over the feasibility of minimizing these differences by special education and training, and whether it is worth devoting considerable resources to doing so. What neither side asks is why (Western) society has been so unwilling to accept and integrate mentally handicapped people, whatever their differences, and why it has treated them in ways which have tended to maximize rather than minimize the differences.

MEDICAL DOMINATION

One version of these differences – the medical version – has had a dominating influence, far outstripping that warranted by the physical conditions that many mentally handicapped people do suffer from. Mental handicap provides a case study of the 'medicalization' of a social problem. It is not, as a recent Royal Commission blandly states, 'an accident of history' that the NHS has such a large responsibility for the mentally handicapped.[10] Rather the reverse: it is a significant historical fact that this has happened, indicative of the way that our society deals with people it finds useless, dangerous, or inconvenient.

Medicine – its institutions, personnel, concepts, and modes of explaining behaviour – has been the main instrument for excluding mentally handicapped people from society. It is not just that hospitals have had to cope with people whom society has rejected, which is how many nurses and doctors see their role. It is also that the medical profession has sanctioned this rejection by producing a whole way of thinking that justifies it. To categorize mentally handicapped people as 'defective' or 'subnormal' is to describe them entirely in terms of their supposed pathology, what is wrong with *them*. Such descriptions effectively mask other aspects of their social existence, or even deny them one at all. The way that we, as a society, behave towards them is left entirely out of account, and in this sense medicine performs an important ideological function. Furthermore, the medical profession has knowingly administered a most deplorable standard of life to the mentally handicapped people in its care. The lack of protest from within the medical profession about this has undoubtedly been aided by the fact that they are seen, in strict medical terms, as incurable and therefore hopeless.

To claim, as will be argued more fully, that medicine has far exceeded its legitimate role, to the detriment of the people involved, is not in any way to deny that there are important, sometimes over-riding, physical factors involved in mental handicap. Biological damage is a brute fact of much mental handicap. Links between mental and physical defects have long been observed. The early writers on idiocy gave as much prominence to the bodily appearance and physical capacities of idiots as they did to their mental abilities. Mental incapacity was almost always seen as stemming from some kind of physical abnormality, although the nature and cause of the latter were seldom known. It was only in the second half of the nineteenth century, with the collecting together of idiots in the first public asylums, that systematic medical interest began.

One of the main areas of medical investigation has been, and is still, the description and classification of different types and syndromes of mental handicap. Many different types have now been identified, but most of these are exceedingly rare. The single most common type is Down's syndrome, or mongolism; no other identifiable syndrome occurs with such frequency.[11] Mental handicap is now usually classified according to the developmental process that is thought to have gone wrong, and/or the stage of embryonic life that is affected. The different syndromes, to name but a few of the main categories, include: inborn errors of metabolism; chromosomal disorders; gross neurological defects; infections and toxic agents during pregnancy and perinatal brain damage.[12]

Despite the century of effort that has gone into such medical investigation, it is still not possible to give a full or precise diagnosis as to the type of mental handicap in more than *one-third* of the instances of severe handicap. The diagnosable proportion is lower still with milder handicap.[13] In very many instances the type of mental handicap is simply unknown, although associated factors may well be identified, for example, mother's age, small birth weight, prolonged birth. In even fewer cases is it possible to identify a precise cause, or to describe the causal mechanisms involved in such a way that curative measures can be devised. Cretinism and phenylketonuria are two of the few exceptions to this.[14]

Some of the physical conditions related to mental handicap are specific to the syndrome in question, such as the distinctive bodily characteristics of Down's syndrome, or of hydrocephalus. Other conditions, such as epilepsy or cerebral palsy, occur with many different types of mental handicap, and also in people who are not mentally handicapped at all. Medical treatment of mental handicap often involves trying to deal with the various physical problems, for example, control of epileptic fits, physiotherapy for spastic conditions, correction of sensory defects, draining of excess fluid in the brain, etc. It also involves the administration of drugs to control behaviour.

There remains a daunting paucity of knowledge about causes and underlying physiological disorders. This can partly be accounted for by the numerous forms in which mental handicap occurs, a reflection of the multitude of processes which can go wrong in the reproduction of human life. The nature of mental handicap is all encompassing – it can express itself in all aspects of a person's being – and this adds to the difficulty of precise description and classification. At the same time there is now sufficient knowledge about social and environmental factors associated with the incidence of mental handicap for more effective preventative measures to be taken. For example, malnutrition of the mother and the foetus is now known to be a significant contributing factor to the incidence of mental handicap, as is poor antenatal and perinatal care of the mother. Mercury poisoning (via ingestion of contaminated food by the mother) and lead poisoning (via direct atmospheric pollution of the child) are both causes of mental handicap that stem directly from the lack of control over industrial and commercial operations. In general, most of the factors correlated with a high incidence of perinatal mortality (for example, socio-economic status, mother's age and health, birth order, the standard of antenatal care) are also associated with mental handicap. Researchers, however, tend to be more interested in investigating the extremely rare but scientifically more definable syndromes (such as metabolic and chromosomal disorders) rather than in trying to promote the social action that would reduce the incidence of the commoner but less clear-cut forms of mental handicap. Other preventative measures, such as the screening of the amniotic fluid of mothers at risk, are still not as widely available as they could be (though it should be noted that such measures are not themselves entirely risk-free).[15]

Yet, within medicine, mental handicap has a very low status. As the recent Royal Commission on the NHS commented: 'Recruitment of doctors is poor both in quantity and quality.' A leading medical journal recently described how subnormality specialists are often recruited from adult-psychiatry failures, the doctors who were not good enough to do anything else.[16] There are very few prestigious careers in this field, relatively few consultantships, and no lucrative private practices. Doctors in general are given very little instruction in mental handicap, despite the fact that general practitioners inevitably will have to deal with mentally handicapped people and their families.[17]

Low status of this kind similarly applies to subnormality

nursing. Recruiting and retaining sufficient good staff has been a persistent problem.* Trainees have often been rejects from general nursing, and the wastage amongst student nurses has been very high.[18] In the 1950s and 60s this led to extensive importation of nursing assistants from abroad, to fill the jobs no one else would take; it was one of the few jobs for which a work permit was not needed. Recently, with higher national unemployment, these problems have become less acute, although they have by no means disappeared.

The low status of mental handicap within medicine is reflected in the proportion of resources allocated to these hospitals. The amount of money spent per patient is lower in handicap hospitals than in any others, including long-stay ones. It amounts to roughly one-third of that spent in acute and general hospitals. And this extraordinary disproportion is not just accounted for by differing medical and nursing provision: even the cost of food per patient is much lower in handicap hospitals than in all others.[19] The ratio of doctors and specialist staff to patients is also extremely low.[20]

Medical knowledge and medical care, then, are of very limited benefit to mentally handicapped people themselves. What expertise exists certainly does not justify the spending of so much of their lives in hospital. Surveys have found that less than one-third of the people in hospital required specialist nursing care: nearly two-thirds (including the children) could walk, were not severely incontinent, required little or no help with washing, dressing or feeding, and had no severe behaviour difficulties.[21] Many of the genuinely medical needs of mentally handicapped people are similar to those of the rest of the population, or to other disabled people, and there is a strong case for arguing that these should be met through the general health service rather than in specialist hospitals. What many handicapped people do need is support and training in their daily lives, and this is not something the medical professions are particularly equipped to provide.

* See Chapter 3.

SOCIAL EXCLUSION

Hospitals tend to function now as places of last resort, when all other alternatives have failed, although this has not always been their function. The exclusion of mentally handicapped people from a life outside hospital is reflected in three main areas of life: the family, education and work. A brief consideration of these in relation to mentally handicapped people will show better than any technical description just what the definition of 'mental handicap' is, and thus what role medicine as a whole has come to play.

The family

The presence of a mentally handicapped person in a family is almost always problematic in some way. Faced with an unusually difficult child, or a highly dependent adult, many families cannot cope or only do so at immense cost to themselves. Families who do keep their handicapped child at home often face a general lowering of their living standards: lower income, because of the mother's inability to go out to work, and/or the presence of a non-wage-earner; over-crowding or unsuitable accommodation; social isolation; fewer holidays or outings.[22] This is quite apart from the extra work involved in looking after a handicapped child, which can seem like ordinary childhood magnified and prolonged a hundred times; or coping with the various emotional and behavioural problems that can arise. Yet, overwhelmingly, hospitalization is seen as a mainly negative choice, inevitable when the particular problems of the family have become too great.[23] What is remarkable is the number of families who do keep their child at home in the face of overwhelming odds, and the many more who would do so if greater practical support (such as domestic help, 'baby' sitting arrangements, short-term relief) were available.

It comes as no surprise to learn that one of the most important factors determining hospitalization is the age and health of the mother.[24] She is usually the person in the family most affected. Not finding it easy to either grow up or grow away, the 'eternal children', as they are sometimes called, can lock their mothers in a never-ending maternal role.

A mentally handicapped person shows up both the strengths and the weaknesses of the nuclear family in our society. The social isolation – the lack of outside support from the state, or of shared responsibility with relatives, neighbours or friends – can make a handicapped child an impossible burden. Even so, the care and affection and the continuing concern that such a child receives in its own family is seldom found elsewhere. One of the sad truths of hospital life is that many people there are suffering from loss of their family, either by death, distance or by being 'put away', and from the failure of the hospital to provide adequate substitute relationships.

Very few mentally handicapped people can hope for a family life of their own, and sexual relationships are often made very difficult for them. Marriage is often discouraged and sterilization encouraged by people in positions of authority over them. This exclusion from marriage and from a full sexual life is common in all societies for which we have any information.[25] Mentally handicapped people are the victims of all kinds of inaccurate stereotypes. They are regarded as sexually promiscuous, or incapable of any kind of sexual activity, or too unstable to keep a marriage together.

Hundreds of thousands of mentally handicapped people have been segregated into hospitals and into single-sex wards during this century, in the belief that this would reduce the number of such people in the population. Many mentally handicapped women have been put into hospitals under custody, purely on the grounds of giving birth to an illegitimate child. The belief that 'most retardates are not good material for parenthood' is still influential, put forward by those who advocate eugenic control (usually sterilization) to reduce the numbers of mentally handicapped people in the population.[26] Yet only a relatively small proportion of such people have mentally handicapped parents: there are many other more significant causes on which attention could be brought to bear. Only in the last decade has there been any attempt to assert the rights of mentally handicapped people to enjoy some freedom of sexual expression.[27]

Education

For families the dependency of mentally handicapped people is the main issue; in schools it is their intelligence. For most of their history mentally handicapped people have either not been educated at all, or else have been educated in special schools and classes, or in hospital. Until 1971, severely handicapped children were legally excluded from education and from the provisions of the 1944 Education Act. They either received some training in occupation centres, or nothing at all. Even now some children in hospital receive extremely little education or training.[28]

Central to the act of exclusion from ordinary school is the IQ test. It is no accident that IQ tests were invented at the beginning of this century, soon after the imposition of national standards of attainment in schools – standards that every child had to meet each year. The tests were originally devised to identify children who were unlikely to benefit from the education offered and who would be likely to hold back the other children if they were kept in the same classes.

The intelligence quotient – as is now widely recognized – is firmly tied to educational and cultural criteria. (This is not of course how psychologists have tended to see it, preferring instead some notion of 'pure' intelligence.) This cultural underpinning implies that the common definition of the mentally handicapped, as those with an IQ of less than 70, largely reflects how well they fit into the prevailing educational system. Failure to do so may reflect as much the nature of the schools – their criteria for adequate performance, their resources, their teaching methods and assumptions, the degree of conformity required – as it does the capacities of the children. Particularly important in success or failure at school is the degree of linguistic, social and cultural conflict involved.

The IQ test was initially hailed as a great scientific discovery because it provided a supposedly objective diagnostic instrument. It led in the early part of this century to the 'discovery' of many more mentally deficient people than had been thought existed. They swelled the category of the 'feeble-minded', and this fuelled the demands for their permanent segregation from the communities they had been living in. Thousands of children, who are in fact no problem to their families and who are living quite adequately in their own sub-cultures, are still defined as mentally handicapped by IQ tests and by the educational system, and are thus sent to special schools. This is particularly true of immigrant groups in a population (for example, West Indian children in Britain or Mexican ones in America), but it also applies to indigenous working-class people, whose family background and social situation may be in complete conflict with the values and methods of the school.[29] It is in this way that the educational system can be said to *produce* mentally handicapped people, who then become the targets for the racial and class attacks of those who believe that IQ is mostly inherited.

Differences between individuals also tend to be maximized rather than minimized within our education system. It is the performance of each individual that counts, not of the whole class. Someone is needed to be bottom of the class, and competition rather than co-operation between children is encouraged from a very early age.[30]

Differences are further amplified by the inferior nature of much of the education that mentally handicapped people receive. Until recently, they had second-rate facilities and badly-paid staff, compared to other schools. It might be thought they need more, not less, education than other children; but in fact they spend fewer hours in school each day, and receive only the legal minimum of years' schooling. Despite the fact that they develop more slowly, their education – by contrast with that of many 'normal' children – stops short at sixteen. It is therefore hardly surprising that some handicapped people complain that they were never given adequate opportunity to learn to read and write. For their schooling often stops just at the point when they are ready to develop these skills: and many of their problems in living independently stem from this disadvantage.

Education in the broader sense is vital if mentally handicapped people are to gain any freedom and self-sufficiency for themselves. It can help provide the skills and confidence that they need, the means to greater control over their own lives. Many of the more progressive thinkers in the field have based their vision of the greater integration of mentally handicapped people into society on the promise of what education, and advances in educational methods, could offer them. This was the spirit in which the first residential schools and public asylums, the precursors of our present hospitals, were set up, in the mid-nineteenth century. Their subsequent development, however, was marked by the demise of educational ideas within them.* We are now witnessing a renewal of educational optimism about mentally handicapped people, and this is increasingly incorporated in contemporary ideas about the reform of hospitals.†

Work

Very few mentally handicapped children can find work when they leave school, yet having a job is as important to them as it is to anyone else. Work represents a passport to economic independence and to 'normality'. However all mentally handicapped people are in an extremely weak position on the labour market; they either cannot sell their labour at all, or only at extremely low rates of pay. They are very vulnerable to the general level of unemployment, often functioning as an unorganized reserve of workers, pleased to have any work they can get. The jobs they do get are usually the worst-paid ones (for example, washing up, cleaning, packing).

Conditions of work within hospitals and Adult Training Centres are even worse. Long hours spent on domestic tasks or industrial contract work are rewarded by only token amounts of pay – £2 a week, for example. Often the economy of the hospital or training centre depends on this supply of cheap or free labour; many local authorities, for example, demand that their centres are economically self-sufficient. At the same time, work is seen as

* See Chapter 5.   † See Chapter 6.

'therapy' or 'training', regardless of its actual content or benefit to the individual worker.[31] And willingness to work, or good performance on the job, are often part of the criteria for release from hospital, despite the extremely repetitive and unstimulating nature of the work itself.

As their labour in hospitals and training centres shows, mentally handicapped people can perform many industrial tasks (for example, simple assembly, sorting and packing) quite competently. Where they are often at a disadvantage is in the initial learning of a task. Many employers are unwilling to allow the extra time needed to instruct them, even though their subsequent performance would match that of other workers. The greatest problems, however, arise from all the other aspects of work: travelling there; arriving punctually; handling money; dealing with unexpected incidents and with the other people at work.[32] It is in all these areas that mentally handicapped people need most support and where they are at the greatest disadvantage.

Only when it is clearly in their economic interests, are employers prepared to facilitate the employment of mentally handicapped people. One advantage that they do have, and that employers are increasingly realizing, is that they are likely to be much less 'trouble' as employees – they tend not to be involved in trade unions, they are prepared to work hard at extremely repetitive tasks, they are less often absent from work than other employees.[33] As one manager of a food processing factory said: 'My (*sic*) mentally handicapped people – 10 per cent of the workforce – make production scheduling more dependable.'[34] Add to this the fact that many handicapped people are desperate to get and keep a job, and it will be seen how readily exploitable they are, when they are 'allowed' to work.

Many myths surround the issue of work and mental handicap. We are often warned that the 'economic burden' of mental handicap will increase as more and more people fail to meet the demands of an increasingly complex and technological society. In this view, mentally handicapped people are the inevitable casualties of economic and technological growth, doomed to be unproductive and dependent. It is clearly true that the nature of our society exacerbates the problem of mental handicap, but not primarily for these reasons. Most people's work has, if anything, become simpler – deskilled – during this century. Technological advances, and the need for greater control by management over the processes of production, have meant that many complex and skilled operations have been broken down into short repetitive sequences.[35] The level of competence required for such work is relatively low, the resulting boredom and frustration very high. Ever increasing speed-ups add further stresses.

The comparative study of mental handicap in different societies has hardly begun, but we do know that all societies have their incompetent and handicapped members, mildly as well as severely so. The 'simple people for simple societies' view wrongly assumes that mentally handicapped people are not such a problem in 'less developed' societies because the level of competence required is not so great as in more 'advanced' ones. This imperialistic assumption is highly questionable. Reading and writing, for example, are skills which have to be formally learned, and without these skills people in our society are highly disadvantaged and liable to score a very low IQ. But by what criteria do we judge that these skills are necessarily more complex or difficult to learn than recognizing, tracking and killing fast-moving animals in a dense forest, or participating in an intricate belief system of myths and symbols?

Furthermore, the economic burden of a handicapped person may be much greater in a so-called 'simple' society that tries to glean a living from a harsh environment. Research in fact shows that there is no straightforward relationship between the harshness of living conditions and how handicapped people are treated.[36] Some very poor societies kill off their handicapped members, others do not. Certainly economic surplus does not guarantee a better life for mentally handicapped people. The richest society in the world, the USA, often seems far more concerned about the economic cost of mentally handicapped people than it does about the degradation it subjects them to.

The production of large numbers of mildly handicapped people cannot be dissociated from other aspects of production in so-called 'advanced' societies. The high rate of mental retardation in the USA parallels the high rate of unemployment there. Chronic and acute unemployment, and the existence of a large sub-section of the population which will work intermittently for extremely low wages with no job security, are endemic features of advanced capitalist societies. These same sub-sections of the population, distinguished by their class or ethnic position, are unlikely to acquire the skills necessary for fuller participation in the society, and it is clear that society could not accommodate all of them if they did. But to blame these people – or their supposedly low IQs – for their lack of success at school or work is tantamount to blaming unemployed people – or their supposedly lazy and scrounging natures – for their failure to work in a society where unemployment is rife.

MEDICAL IDEOLOGIES

We have seen how the exclusion of mentally handicapped people from so many aspects of life has resulted in their incarceration in hospitals, despite the fact that their needs are not primarily medical. Their exclusion from society is also reflected in the ways that they are seen and thought about, and this applies as much to handicapped people outside hospitals as it does to those inside. Medical domination reaches beyond the actual institutions into what we may call 'medical model' thinking. This involves a particular way of explaining behaviour: people are seen primarily in terms of what is wrong or abnormal about them, rather than in terms of the environment they live in, the way other people behave towards them, or their needs arising from this. Interactions between people, both past and present, or the social context of a situation, tend to be discounted in favour of some kind of defect within the person. Learning difficulties, for example, will tend to be phrased in terms of someone's incapacities – their inability to generalize, their poor attention – rather than in terms of the instructor's inadequacies, the deficiencies of the layout or of the material to be learned. Sexual behaviour is often seen as 'promiscuity due to mental subnormality', rather than as a valid desire for physical and emotional contact in a highly depriving situation, such as a single-sex ward.

Medical model thinking tends to support the status quo. The subnormality of the individual, rather than the subnormality of the environment, tends to be blamed for any inadequacies. Rather than alter some aspect of the environment or question other people's behaviour, the usual remedy is to try to change or suppress the individual's behaviour. Within most institutions staff have a vested interest in not questioning the quality of the patients' environment too radically, since they themselves are part of that environment.[37] By focusing on the abnormal and hopeless nature of the patients, their own behaviour remains unchallenged.

Similar kinds of explanation are also apparent in many of the theories that psychology has produced about mentally handicapped people. 'Defect' theories, for example, have flourished. These attempt to identify and analyse the differences between mentally handicapped and normal people in terms of specific defects the former are supposed to have: slow reaction times, inconsistent learning strategies, inadequate short-term memories, and many more. All such theories emphasize how mentally handicapped people are different and inferior compared to others; there is much less emphasis on how they are similar. There is also very little psychological work on what sense of themselves mentally handicapped people have, and how they cope with being handicapped; nor is there very much interest in trying to relate the behaviour and attitudes of mentally handicapped people to the way that other people interact with them. To try to capture their experience of the world would bring out points of identification, needs that they share with others.

Focusing on the differences between people, in preference to the similarities, is a form of exclusion – an exclusion from the possibility of a shared reality. In this way our common ways of thinking about mentally handicapped people reflect society's exclusion of them from any shared life. Mental hospitals embody this exclusion, and in doing so they exaggerate rather than reduce the differences between handicapped people and the rest of society.

Whenever we listen to them, mentally handicapped people

make us aware of their sense of exclusion, of their desire to leave hospital and live more like other people do:

My business is to get away, right away altogether so I can forget all about my lifetime in the past. You can't help thinking about it because you're still in the same county as the hospital where you was. You must get right away, so you could forget. I'm looking forward to the future, that's what my ambition is, to get things organized if I can.[38]

One survey in a hospital found that three-quarters of the patients (interviewed by a doctor) wanted to live elsewhere.[39] Most of these would have preferred to live with relatives, but when given the choice of hostel or hospital, the majority chose a hostel. Another study of ex-patients living in the community found that freedom from the institution was the primary goal for every participant, and that they all had a deep sense of shame and stigma from living there. 'I never belonged there in the first place.'[40] For many mentally handicapped people, hospital represents an intolerable restriction on their freedom to do the very ordinary things that most people take for granted: deciding when to go to bed and get up, what to wear, who to be with, whether or not to go out, how to spend leisure time. 'I don't have my own life in there.'[41]

Being so excluded, it is not surprising that normality is a burning issue in the lives of many mentally handicapped people. It is increasingly becoming an important issue for those who care for them. It may be the most articulate who tell us most about the pain of being categorized as mentally handicapped, but we cannot assume that the less articulate are any less aware of their differences. Many normal people mistakenly believe that mentally handicapped people cannot 'tell the difference', and do not know what they are missing. Such an attitude protects us rather than them. It protects us from having to experience the pain of mentally handicapped people about the life they have to endure. It protects us from having to act on the consequences that a full awareness of such a reality would bring. It is mystifying as well as patronizing to suppose that mentally handicapped people are not aware of their differences from others, because it denies them any valid perception of their own situation and their own reality. It is also a way of perpetuating those differences.

There is no simple solution to the fundamental problem of difference. We cannot deny that important differences amongst people exist, nor suppose that they are only a matter of arbitrary social labels.[42] But this does not mean that we should exaggerate and reinforce these differences, as we do, nor see them as entirely due to the deficient nature of the individuals concerned. What is needed, but seems so hard to achieve, is a recognition of difference amongst people that allows for special needs and unusual behaviour, but which doesn't thereby disqualify anyone from full acceptance as a human being. 'To each according to his [her] needs, from each according to his [her] abilities' – mentally handicapped people make more demands than any other people do on the humanity implicit in this idea, and our desire to put it into practice.

Chapter 2

Everyday Life on the Ward

by FRANK THOMAS

I saw the advertisement for the job in my local paper: 'Do you want to work with the mentally subnormal? No experience necessary – we will train you.'

'I couldn't work with those sort of people'; 'You're doing a wonderful job, you must have such courage.' These are frequent reactions from people who have little or no contact with the mentally handicapped, severely subnormal, educationally subnormal, call them what you will.

I worked with them at the hospital for over six months and what follows are the impressions I received over that time. A daily record, but interspersed with hindsights, opinions, conclusions. A great deal is not very tasteful. But then it is not a very tasteful situation. It is written as I felt it at the time – crude, vulgar, sometimes obscene. It may offend your sensibilities. It should do.

The diary mainly concerns one particular ward, or 'villa', as they were called in the hospital. It is not an exposé or a vendetta against anyone in particular, but against a system staffed by vulnerable individuals. The purpose of this diary is to use a local example to highlight a national problem. Focusing on one particular hospital, ward, or member of staff can divert attention from similar situations and make it seem an exception rather than the general picture. The fact that the ward in question was considered a soft option at the hospital and not a 'nasty' ward, only serves to highlight the appalling nature of the situation generally.

The nursing officer who interviewed me was more interested in the idea that I was not using my educational qualifications than in assessing my suitability as a potential nursing assistant.*

* Frank had spent two years at college on a course for teaching the mentally handicapped before working at the hospital.

'*You don't want to be a nursing assistant all your life, now do you?*' he remarked.

On my way in I had noticed what seemed to be a sheltered workshop, which I mistook for the local adult training centre. '*Oh, our patients will never aspire to those heights,*' he said. '*They're much lower than that.*'

On the day I started, the charge nurse on the ward commented that I had an easy number here, not a lot of trouble, not much violence. A guy who started work on the same day threw in a few comments to the effect that he wouldn't stand any nonsense, any patient '*coming it over him*' would get what for.

Thus my first impressions of the hospital, staff-wise, were ones of apprehension, visions of a thousand bodies considered useless by the nursing officer and as potential punch-bags by a nursing assistant, of the job as a soft option by the charge nurse – violence, or the absence of it, the key to it all.

* * *

When you first enter the hospital it seems a peaceful place – a wide path leading to the main building, trees lining well-kept banks of grass, the majority of buildings solid and imposing two-storey blocks, built to last for ever. A few people are walking about with varying degrees of urgency, some staring ahead, some talking loudly to themselves, others cadging cigarettes, demanding your name, offering their own. Nurses in long white coats pushing wheelchairs. A strange place for the first time, in many ways much more pleasant than hospitals for the physically sick, each ward possessing its own stretch of greenery, and trees everywhere.

Over all there is a lot of space – but then nearly a thousand people live, eat, sleep, play and work here. Only when you go on the wards do you realize how small and cramped everything really is. This is where the patients spend most of their time – around forty patients and eight or so staff of various kinds – the walls closing in on you. From inside the ward you can see the green and the trees through the thick windows, access to them only with a key. Only the staff had keys.

* * *

My first vivid impression of the ward itself was the smell. An unpleasant mixture of urine and faeces.

' *You'll get used to that,' smiles the charge nurse.*

I was fitted out with a couple of white coats and the laundry system was carefully explained to me. I was led down the side of the ward – huge old-fashioned beige radiators, beige walls. The day-room was an expanse of green flooring, with plastic chairs stacked against six-seater tables. A woman was furiously mopping the floor, staring at us as we walked over it. The colour telly filled the far left-hand corner with rows of easy chairs facing it, like a mini-cinema. The door at the end of the day-room led into the room where those who were not considered good enough to go to occu-pational therapy or to the patient activity centre passed their days.

I was next shown the shower-room and toilets – cold floors, high ceilings, glaring lights, a row of lavatories with no doors. Then the morning-room – dark brown lockers full of raincoats and overcoats, the majority dun-coloured and buttonless. In another locked cup-board, the shaving gear, brushes and combs. Upstairs, next to the new clothes-cupboard, was a locked room with nothing in it – the room for patients who became too hot to handle.

Through the next door was the H-shaped dormitory. Uniformity was not in it: the only concessions to individuality were the dark brown lockers, and the 'personalized' nylon bedspreads. There was nothing on the walls, the whole scene an abstract pattern of brown wood, pastel nylon, green floor, beige walls. Hiding in one corner, muttering incessantly, was Derek, an older patient.

*   *   *

Breakfast. *Arriving at the villa just after first light was a very strange, unnerving experience. Unsuspectingly I rang the bell, chatting to David who was also waiting to get in, having done the laundry. No one came. Through the small windows some lads could be seen moving around in slow motion, as if in a trance; every now and again a grinning face pressed against the window, laughing. The lads were trying to get out, we were trying to get in. Only another staff had the key to let me in, not any of the residents. Eventually when I was in, it was a place where at that moment I had no wish to be – along with a lot of the lads, if the truth be known.*

Nurse: '*Hello, shitface, here's your sodding breakfast.*'

Charge nurse: '*Tables! Come on, you lot! Get yourselves to your seats! Stand by your seats! Keep quiet. Quiet now! Right, sit down! Green, shut up! What's up with you lot this morning? Any more noise and you'll go to bed at four o'clock. Right, keep the noise down. First table! Come on, get your porridge before it gets cold. Come on, you lazy buggers, we haven't got all day.*'

All this at an ear-splitting level.

'*Tommy Rayner, if you don't come and get it, you won't get any. Move yourself!*'

Tommy: '*Fuck off and leave me alone. I'll get you for this. I'll tell the boss what you're doing to me.*'

One of the residents rises to his feet, totters to the trolley and grabs two bowls of porridge. He slops these down on the table and repeats the procedure. Tea is spilt everywhere, on to the bread, over the butter, into the jam. No one seems to notice or care.

'*Second table, get your porridge! Colin, leave Tommy's bread alone. Look at Colin, the dirty sod, like a bloody animal he is.*'

Colin by this time had buttered, jammed and licked all the bread on his table. And drunk all the tea as well.

'*Tommy, eat your porridge. Don't sit there playing with it. Try to get some in your bloody mouth, not all over the fucking floor.*

'*Martin, what are you doing? Stop playing with it or I'll get your prick out and stir the porridge with it, if you're not careful.*'

'*I don't like this porridge.*' *Eric articulates slowly but deliberately, in a whining voice that suggests he hasn't the energy to carry on much longer.*

Charge nurse: '*It's not my fault, I didn't cook it. You'll just have to eat it and be thankful you get fed every day as it is. Well, don't eat it, give it to Simon. How can they eat this luke-warm shit? Still, it's all the same to them. Stop that, Hodges, stop throwing the water, and do your trousers up, must we keep telling you? We don't want to see what you've got hanging between those skinny legs of yours!*'

'*Why are you crying, Keith?*' *a nurse asks.*

'*I'm hungry.*'

'*How the fuck can you be hungry? You've eaten two bowls of this muck already. Oh, sod you, here's another one, hope it makes you sick.*'

It does. Keith spews over the table, is rushed to the toilet to be cleaned up, still moaning that he is hungry.

'Shut up, you stupid fish-face, McNeil. You're fucking mad.'

'Not mad. You're mad,' *mutters the sickly-looking Keith.*

'What's mad?' *says Derek,* 'What's mad?'

'What's that bloody smell? Someone's shit. Who is it? Who's shit himself? Lewis, you filthy bastard! Go and change your pants and don't ever do that again. You are a filthy lot, don't know why I bother.'

'Right, first table, plates! Get your next load of rubbish.'

* * *

After most of the residents have eaten, the next stage begins. As part of the hospital training programme, the tables are cleared one at a time, the charge nurse barking out orders 'to get the lazy bastards moving'. The crockery has to be placed in certain positions on the trolley – plates on plates, saucers on saucers, slops in the bucket, etc.

Some of the lads have been doing it this way for twenty years now. Some automatically place the crockery correctly, some try hit and miss, others see the whole thing as pointless and shove everything down together. When this happens (usually) the nurse barks out an order: 'Put that cup underneath, you thick or something? Not like that, come back and do it properly.' *Apart from this verbal battering, any straying from the norm can mean a shove, kick or punch.* 'It must be done proper, it's all part of their training.'

* * *

Lunch time. *Charge nurse:* 'Right sit down now and don't anybody dare talk!' *To me:* 'Don't talk to the lads over their dinner, Frank. It only upsets them. The noise level goes up, everybody starts talking. It's so annoying. You should have seen Mr Robbins, the charge nurse who used to be on this villa. He only had to shout once and all the noisy lads would be quiet just like that. No messing. Now look at them. There's always a couple of the bastards talking, never stop they don't. You have to shout at them three times before some of them shut up.'

Another nurse: 'Why should they be quiet when they're eating?'

Charge nurse: 'Of course they should be quiet. It drives you mad otherwise.'

'What if they want to talk? You talk over your dinner.'

'That's different. Ordinary people can talk over their dinner. But these lads, they're so noisy. It does them good to be told to shut up now and again.' More now than again . . .

Meal times are treated as military operations, slick and sick. Any resemblance to a social occasion has now been removed, if there ever was any. The rituals, the discipline and order, may be all right for the army, but not for a home. Meals satisfy only the physiological needs of the patients – they are allowed little or no enjoyment, as the staff's task seems to be to get the business over as quickly as possible. It's just another chore to be overcome.

* * *

Dinner for the lads is at twelve o'clock. They are finished and cleared away in half an hour. For the next forty minutes they are forced to sit at their tables. They do not know why this is. Searching questions to the nurses on the ward reveal the same lack of knowledge.

'Why?' asks Clive. Nobody answers.

'Stop that rocking.' Barry, Colin and Tommy take no notice and rock to and fro, Colin more vigorously than the rest.

* * *

The smell of the toilets infiltrates the food. The food itself is often overcooked, cold and inedible. The precarious journey from the kitchen to the villa means that the soup often spills over into the custard, and vice versa. But it all goes down the same way, so why bother to complain?

David comes up for his dinner. The orderly hands it to him.

'Looks like shit,' she tells him, as he is about to eat his main meal of the day.

* * *

Tea mixed with milk and sugar to save time, mess and trouble. How many lumps, say when with the milk? You must be joking.

'*That bloody cake, they've managed to get more on the sodding floor than in their bleeding mouths.*'

'*I know what you mean. They don't deserve good food. They don't appreciate the difference, so what's the use?*'

*   *   *

Harry Small was asked to call the staff for their tea-break.

'*Tables!*' *shouts Harry, perfectly taking the piss out of the iron summons and those who make it.*

*   *   *

Helping at meal times on my first day nearly drove me into getting my coat and heading for home. Standing at the patients' meal trolley, wearing my crisp white clinical uniform, hearing the high-pitched abuse, the constant shouting at the patients to sit down and shut up, was enough to make me jack it all in on the spot.

There was perhaps one staff, Bruce, who treated the patients as humans, as individuals. In the following days I jolted him out of the apathy and despair he was experiencing with the situation. He at the same time convinced me that if we worked together we might get a few things done. The potentialities of the situation could be exploited only if I chose to stay.

Could I help the lads get through the day without feeling too bad, soften the blows they constantly received, give a more humane aspect to their nursing care? With Bruce's help this seemed possible. The snag was of course that there were the other staff to contend with. What was needed was an attempt to break down the rigid staff/patient dichotomy, to be a friend of the lads, with all that entails. Completely reject the authoritarian side of my role as staff.

All the bizarre happenings on the ward would still go on, but at least I could define a purpose in being there. To stay meant to a certain extent accepting the situation, but at the same time not being part of it – an insider and an outsider simultaneously.

You change. Whether you change the system or the system changes you, you change. Circumstances change to change you. People hit other people. Horrific. A daily occurrence. A norm. You want to vomit at the ever present reek of urine. You get used to it. People swear, defile, bite themselves, scream incessantly, say nothing, do less, go berserk at you, dribble for ever, have dried food all over their clothes, look a terrible grey mess. A superficial overview. You get to know the lads, it doesn't take too long. Each lad is a highly individual person in his own right. Such relationships can be very satisfying, rewarding and enjoyable experiences.

As far as I could, every time I saw a patient being harassed or bullied or abused, I would attempt to relieve the suffering, for suffering it was. And with those lads who were up to it, we discussed their situation freely – the hospital, the staff, the food, what it was all about. It was an opportunity to take a look at their situation for themselves without the other staff interfering, an experience they had not had before. If this smacks of anarchy, well – maybe what these hospitals need is a revolution to sort them out.

* * *

Change at last! *The hospital in its wisdom, after being in operation for nearly fifty years, has decided that it would be a good idea if a degree of 'normality' were gradually introduced on to the wards. A choice of meals was decided on as a good way of getting this going, with each individual patient given the responsibility for collecting his own food.*

This caused consternation amongst the staff:

'They might spill it all over the floor, it's all a waste of time. What was wrong with the old system? Everybody got enough, they even got seconds, nobody grumbled. Leave well enough alone, that's what I say. Let's face it, they're not normal people, the poor sods. All this change, it just confuses them.'

'The people who make these decisions just don't know what they're letting us in for. It only makes more work for us and it doesn't do the patients much good either. They choose something for dinner days before, they don't know what it is, and when they come up and get it they don't even want it, they want something else. You tell them they chose it and they've got to eat it, you start more trouble and no one's any happier.'

'The old way was much better, they got what they were given and that was that. This place is getting worse. If it goes on like this, I'll think about' leaving.

It was bad enough for the staff to adjust to this new system – they had to work much harder to organize both the choice of meals and their distribution. For the patients, after years of 'Get this down you and quick', it was sheer murder. The staff expected them to relate to the new system immediately. The chef seemed to think he was cooking for an ordinary restaurant with an exclusive clientèle. The lads are definitely an exclusive club but not to the extent that they know the ins and outs of 'sauté potatoes', 'fricassé', 'gâteaux', etc.

'What do you want for dinner today, Chris, quiche lorraine, that's a posh egg and bacon pie, or braised liver?' I asked.

'You choose, you're the staff.'

'That's not the point, Chris. You've got a choice. Tell me what you want.'

'You heard me. You choose, you've got the white coat on.'

'Bacon or beans on toast, Benny?'

'Chips, chips,' says Benny.

For a dozen or so of the patients the choice has to be made for them. Some were on diets. Some were echolaic – they always chose the last thing you said; even changing the order round, they still chose the last item. As a conscious policy, the new system was a failure. The resulting meals often bore no resemblance to their written description, other choices looked more appealing, sometimes the kitchen confused the orders. Imagine being asked on a Monday if you'll fancy fried egg for Friday's breakfast and you'll appreciate the limitations. But as a social occasion the lads got a lot from it; discussing their preferences for meals was the most enjoyable part of the day, for me and for them. At least it was a legitimate excuse – because one was needed – to engage in long conversations with the patients and still be seen to be working in the hospital sense. It enabled David Travis to be pinned down and be talked to, even if his choice was echolaic. Each of the lads stamped his own particular personality on the occasion.

'Right lads, let's talk about what we're going to eat on Thursday.'

'What we are going to eat? You're staff, you eat your own food,' says Harry.

'Right, let's talk about what you are going to eat. OK, Harry?'

'OK, what about food?' quips Harry.

'*Breakfast, there's a choice between porridge and cornflakes. What do you fancy, Simon?*'

Simon fingers his chin pensively, tilts his head, rolls his eyes.

'*Let's see, I think I'll have . . . no, changed my mind, I'll have porridge, I like porridge.*'

'*Melvin, what do you want for your breakfast on Thursday, porridge or cornflakes?*'

'*Porridge, yes, porridge. Good for you I've been told, I'll have porridge.*'

'*I'll have cornflakes, Frank, I like cornflakes, you get more milk,*' says Clive.

'*Now, Thursday lunch, let's start with you, Clive. It's cheese pie, boiled beef or fish. And remember your weight.*'

'*Is it fried fish or boiled?*'

'*Fried, Clive.*'

'*Oh, I'll have boiled beef then. Won't get fat on that, will I?*'

Simon was thoughtfully taking in all the information available.

'*Make it fish, I like fish. Fish and chips. Are there chips? I hope so.*'

'*There are chips, Simon, though the cook's given them a funny name. He's called them sauté potatoes for some reason.*'

'*I don't like salty potatoes. Don't like salt at all. Who wants salty potatoes? I'll have fish, potatoes with no salt, and peas,*' says Harry.

'*Tommy, tell us what you'd prefer.*'

'*Read them again,*' says Tommy who knows full well the choices but likes to play along.

'*Chalk, stones or sand. What do you fancy, Tommy?*'

'*Don't play around, Frank. I'll have cheese pie. Sand, you can't eat sand!*'

*Every few minutes while I was talking to this group of lads, Benny leaned across the table and grinned at me. '*Chips,*' he muttered incessantly, '*chips.*'

What price macédoine and fricassé now?

* * *

Bathtime. '*Dry yourself, I'm not drying those scrawny bollocks of yours. I don't know where they've been. Do it yourself, you lazy bastard.*'

'*You don't half look a sight. Look at you, like a load of shit done up in the middle.*'

'*Look at those weird spots on Clive's back. Don't touch them, you might catch something.*'

Clive could hear what was being said about his back and was clearly upset that people, especially nurses, should talk about him in this way.

'*Look at that thing on Simon's tool.*'

'*Oh, that's nothing, it's only a cyst.*'

Eric comes out of the shower. Blood trickles down the inside of both legs.

'*Christ, Eric, what's that?*'

'*It's his piles again, poor sod.*'

'*Can I see the doctor tomorrow?*' says Eric in his slow monotone, resigned to the pain he must be suffering.

The supply of pants runs out – again.

'*Keep your old ones on. Never mind the shit. It didn't bother you before.*'

'*These towels will do. No good dirtying clean ones.*'

'*Where shall I put the dirty linen and these dirty clothes?*'

'*Oh, just chuck them on the floor. Somebody'll pick them up later. You don't want to get any of the shit on your hands, let one of the patients do it. They won't mind.*'

'*Put those shitty pants in the bag. No, in the bag, you dozy bleeder. I don't know, they're all fucking thick today.*'

*   *   *

In the bathroom the smell is really atrocious. The lads' toenails and fingernails seem to smell even after a shower. Hair is washed with really crappy shampoo, never dried, just combed into place wet, even if they are going straight out afterwards. Some of the lads have a strong aversion to clean clothes. They become so attached (sometimes literally, with soiled underwear) to some of their clothes that it is a major operation, not always completely successful, to convince them of the virtues of clean clothes. Brian's feet are in a dreadful state. Because of the admittedly awful stink emanating from them even after a bath, no one, if he could possibly help it, would cut his nails or do something about his corns.

Most of the lads are covered in cuts and bruises of one kind or another – some self-inflicted, some from other patients, some from the staff. Fresh injuries get reported, but what can you actually do about them?

*   *   *

A new style of bathing – after forty years it had been decided that perhaps after all the system in operation has been, to say the least, a trifle degrading for the patients, a bit of a trial for the staff too. Previously all the lads 'down for a bath' just piled into the bathroom, stripped off, and stood there shivering until their name was called. To say the result was chaotic is an understatement. Piles of clothes left on the floor, no one knowing who they belonged to, whether they were clean or dirty. The staff on edge, drying patients who hadn't been bathed. The patients dazed and confused, more often than not still dirty at the end of it all.

Under the new system only three patients are to be allowed in at any one time, and three chairs are to be put in the bathroom for them to place their clothes on and sit on quietly until called. In theory this was great – it was what Bruce, the sympathetic nursing assistant, and I did anyway if we were on our own. The occasion could then develop into a civilized social event.

In practice, a couple of days went by and the old situation re-established itself, chaos reigning once more.

*   *   *

None of the loos have a door on them and a row of lads can be seen squatting on the toilets, in full view of everybody.

For years the situation has been no different, the lads supposedly knowing no better. Bruce suggests it would not be a bad idea if the lads could have a little more privacy in the toilet – doors would not be amiss. Rick, the charge nurse, admits that since the ward was upgraded a couple of years ago, there will be no more money for another five years.

*   *   *

Albert Stern has cancer of the stomach and has been classified as a terminal case. He has been a resident at the hospital for many *years. Everybody feels sorry for Albert and the age-old rule of treating everyone exactly the same is bent a little with Albert. As a concession Albert is now allowed to have a private bath, supervised by a member of staff, with special soap and shampoo. Seems you have to be dying before you can be treated as an individual at the hospital.*

Lying back in the bath, Albert really appreciated the privileged treatment he was receiving.

'The soap's nice, sir, is it special?'

'That's right, Albert, very special, just for you.'

'Is a bath better than a shower, sir?'

'Well, they're both nice, you feel clean after both. But you can't lie back in a shower, can you?'

'No, that's right. A bath is much nicer. This soap's very nice.'

Albert breaks into a couple of songs from 'The Sound of Music', and we chat for ages about his love of musicals, his interest in being kidnapped, and the positive advantages of one soap over another. Albert's independent air before being bathed, of asking for the harsh bathmat inside the bath to be removed before he would consent to get in, is a great part of his personality. If he doesn't like or agree with anything, you are left in no doubt. It's a trait the hospital policy is always trying to eradicate from residents' make-up, yet at the same time they are always pressing for more 'suitable' candidates for bungalow training.

* * *

Getting dressed. 'This'll do. He'll never know the difference.'

A coat covered in stains with no buttons. The coat in question would fit someone a foot taller and several stone heavier. Simon looked a terrible sight.

'I'd like one with buttons,' he said.

'We've got no time to sort one out specially for you. Take this one.'

'It's too big.'

'Never mind that. It'll keep you warm.'

To another nurse: 'Where've you been, Ray?'

'Been trying to find a pair of pants to fit Terry.'

'*Bloody hell. If it'd been me I'd have left him with none on – it's a nice enough day.*'

* * *

Bad habit I picked up from the other nurses. Fitting out someone for his trip to the workshop and muttering '*That'll do*', as if the guy's appearance meant nothing to him, just a neat reproduction of my own preferences or lack of them. Not asking the guy if he was all right, whether it'll do. If a person is not allowed a say in what he looks like, then what is the point?

Haircuts en masse – short back and sides, no one is allowed to refuse. Choice of raincoat from a communal pile, communal underwear and socks. Communal combs and brushes. One tube of toothpaste and a couple of tooth mugs for twenty-five patients.

* * *

Panic about dressing the lads for a visit home. It doesn't seem to matter whether the lads dress like tramps on the villa, but it would be a reflection on the nursing care given if patients were to arrive home less than tidy. The lads are shoved into anything every morning, especially if they happen to be staying on the ward all day long. If they go to the workshops, the patient activity centre, or occupational therapy, then their appearance matters a little more. If they're in a situation where the outside world actually gets to look at them, then tidiness and smartness assume paramount importance.

All this time there is a surplus of new clothes in the store cupboard. Nurses are loath to distribute it: '*What's the point? They'll only mess it up.*'

* * *

Lawrence talks constantly of the suit he wants to buy. If these lads didn't have such an obsession about possessing a good suit – an obsession that society as it used to be, continued unbroken in the hospital, has given them – then they could own some excellent clothes. Nothing is more depressing than seeing forty suit-clad men all wearing the same slippers sitting round watching flickers on a TV screen. The suits they buy give them no change out of £30 or more and they only wear them at most three or four times a week, for a few hours at a time. The same amount of money would fit them out with jumpers, shirts, jeans – a variety that would break down the institutional effects of the clothes they do wear.

*   *   *

Experts. *The hospital boasts a psychology department. It has now employed a third member of staff, a psychological assistant (PA). His assignment on the villa was to study the behaviour of Colin. Colin showed what were considered bizarre behavioural symptoms: rocking on his chair, eating the other patients' food, eating tobacco, patting himself on the head to the accompaniment of all manner of noises, attempting to twist his head off the top of his neck, bouncing up and down – to name but a few.*

The PA's task was to act as a 'participant observer', which suggests he should merge into the running of the ward so as to observe Colin without Colin's knowledge. Possibly the whole exercise was pointless anyhow, since the PA had only one day to make his observations. Not a very extensive amount of information on which to base a whole programme for the 'correction of behaviour'.

If the PA had been really trying to blend in with the staff on the ward, wouldn't he have noticed that one common factor was the wearing of a white coat? To make himself really noticeable as a newcomer, he wore a suit of conspicuous colour and no white coat. The stack of paper about two feet long and the pen he carried all contributed to Colin's identification of him as an intruder. The PA stood about four feet from Colin and commenced to record his observations.

Colin fixed him with a stare and sat stock still, displaying none of his usual 'symptoms'. He just sat there, quiet as a mouse, staring at his participant observer in disbelief.

Every time Colin actually rose from his seat and walked a few paces, the PA followed him religiously, scratching away with his pen and paper as if an invisible length of elastic linked them both. After about half an hour, Colin decided to break loose from his participant observer. He began to walk very fast towards the entrance of the ward, the PA following. Once at the entrance Colin ran and ran, the PA breaking into a kind of gallop behind him. Knots of people stood still to observe these two beings in full flight, the sound of raucous laughter echoing round the wards.

Colin finally settled in the patient activity centre. The *P A* arrived, red in the face and sweating profusely. He began to write. Colin sat very still and was the model of what most nurses believe to be a good patient – absolutely quiet and immobile, no trouble at all. What the *P A* found to write is a little beyond me, but write he did. Half an hour later and still scribbling, the *P A* followed Colin back to the villa for lunch.

Kath (a nurse) whispered to Elsie (an orderly) not to shout abuse at the patients whilst the intruder was present. All through lunch Colin kept his incredible behaviour going. He ate only his own dinner. At the end of the session the *P A* said he didn't really see the problem with Colin. As soon as he had gone, Colin reverted to his usual self.

Bruce became quite concerned about Colin and his habit of wolfing down every dog-end, every bit of tobacco he could find, even lighted cigarettes. He tried to start a programme aimed at breaking Colin of this habit. Although it hadn't done Colin any harm, this habit was disturbing for the other lads on the ward who were always the object of Colin's attentions when he found he must have tobacco to eat. He was never less than violent if the particular recipient of his attention was unwilling to co-operate.

Kath, with an air of boredom, said, 'Oh, don't bother, Bruce, it's all been tried before. I wouldn't waste your time, you'll get nothing to show for it.' Kath was watching the *TV* as she said this. Bruce gave up, his motivation shattered by this hostility.

*   *   *

Case conference. *It has been organized as usual to discuss those patients who were giving the most trouble to the staff and the rest of the patients. The docile, non-communicative ones, those who kept themselves to themselves, were largely ignored, never the subject of any inter-disciplinary meeting.*

The doctor inquires about Colin, suggests that the increased dosage of high-powered tranquillizers should be continued if no side-effects are noticed. Rick quips that as opposed to side-effects, the drugs had no effects at all. Thus Colin would continue on a drug

*regime enough to dose four people up to the eyeballs with no dis-
cussion as to what long-term effects this may have on him. The
doctor reigned supreme, nobody questioned his actions, only carried
out his orders.*

*Seems that Colin's habit of eating tobacco started a mere six
months ago, but the general consensus was that it was now so
firmly part of his behaviour that it was a permanent fixture. The
psychologist's reaction was similar to his reaction to Nicky Taverne,
that if it didn't do him any harm then leave it at that: 'If he can
communicate his needs effectively without verbalizing, then perhaps
only harm can come in encouraging him to verbalize. At the very
least an acute sense of frustrations at his limited speech would, if
used to communicate with, create a time lag between request and
receipt.' Hardly very supportive for nurses who want to encourage
some measure of independence or some semblance of social skills in
their patients.*

Chapter 3

Care or Control?

A hospital is a world divided into two, where the staff dominate the patients and the patients are dependent on the staff for most of their needs. Each patient's conduct is continually open to judgement. The staff themselves are subject to a rigid and divisive hierarchy.

In such a world opposition is extremely difficult; the hospital's social structure itself serves to reinforce the dependence and incapacity of patients. Complaints by patients (or their relatives) do not get beyond ward level unless corroborated by a member of staff. And if the staff complain about specific incidents or about conditions in general, they may well put their promotion prospects or their jobs at risk.[1]

These are circumstances in which it becomes easy to objectify people. Objectification occurs in relationships where people are treated more like things than like persons. It leads to the denial of certain qualities they have, or it is thought they should have, as people. There is clearly enormous scope for discussing what these qualities are, what 'as people' means.[2] It is often easier to identify the absence of these qualities than their presence. Equally it is often easier to describe situations which are objectifying, invalidating or even brutalizing, rather than those in which people are clearly respected 'as people'.

For present purposes we can assume that some of the main absences in objectifying relationships are: the absence of any equality or of any similarity between people; the absence of the possibility that people can be anything other than prescribed by their social roles or definitions; the absence of the acknowledgement of subjectivity, of people's own consciousness of themselves. In the world of the hospital, all these values are denied, as this chapter describes. Whatever the intention of individuals to the contrary, it is a dehumanized world, a world where the maximum amount of objectification has become almost inevitable.

Only against such a background of dehumanization is it possible for a nurse to say of his work: 'I never give up on a subject. I get a good response because I treat them like human beings.'[3] Such a statement from a nurse should hardly be necessary. That it is necessary reveals how very precarious is the patients' status as people, how frequently they are in danger of not being considered human beings like the rest of us.

Stating the issues in this way, however, does not mean that the question is merely one of personal morality within any given hospital. It is not just a matter of staff somehow respecting patients more or being 'nicer' to them. Nor, as is often assumed, are the problems only those of resources – of providing better material conditions and more workers. These are extremely important considerations but they are not what fundamentally determines the nature of staff–patient relationships. For these are the relationships of a society within a society – the society of the hospital, with its own structure and dynamics, within that society which originally created it.

To understand these relationships we have to look at the material and social realities within which the staff have to work. For it is within a framework of 'work' for the staff that relationships with patients are constructed. It is important, therefore, to explore what 'work' means to the staff and how they see themselves as workers, as well as seeing the patients as the work to be done.

MANAGEMENT

An overwhelming reality in all hospitals is the inadequate number of staff in relation to the number of patients. One of the most frequently mentioned problems of mental handicap hospitals, this condition is often used to explain all other acknowledged deficiencies. Shortage of staff seems to occur whatever the economic climate – either because recruitment is difficult in times of relatively high employment or because, as now, cut-backs in health service funding mean that many posts are not filled. Perhaps the most frequent demand of all the different nursing organizations is for an increase in staff, particularly qualified ones.[4]

To quote an average figure for overall staff–patient ratios is nevertheless fairly meaningless: numbers of staff actually on duty depend on the time of day, the type of ward, the hospital allocation policy, sickness, overtime, rest-breaks, etc. But it is not uncommon to find a ward with thirty patients and two or three nursing staff; the maximum number of nursing staff on duty seldom exceeds five or six, even with the most handicapped patients. Acute crises can occur when one nurse may find herself in sole charge. Often there is uncertainty about how many staff will actually be on duty on a particular shift.

Furthermore, most staff members on any one ward are only there temporarily. Anything from a half to two-thirds of the staff are 'floaters' – student nurses in training, untrained nursing assistants moved from other wards, college students on vacation jobs, etc. Even 'permanent' staff can be fairly temporary, sometimes working on one particular ward for no more than three or four months.

The results of this situation are illustrated by the findings of one study: on a ward for profoundly handicapped patients, 80 different nursing staff had worked on the day shifts during a six-month period; on another ward for mildly handicapped women, 123 different staff had worked during a year and a half.[5] The charge nurses tend to be the most permanent ward staff: the untrained student nurses are the most temporary and these are the ones who have most direct contact with patients. Thus, although most wards have a relatively stable group of patients, there is a constantly changing and insufficient population of nurses. It is not surprising that control becomes a paramount issue for the staff.

Rick, the charge nurse: 'These people from outside they only see the patients once or twice. No idea what we have to put up with. They haven't got to work here. They might think a bit differently then, understand why we do the things we do, say the things we say. We aren't cruel. But to survive, to make the system fair to every-

body, we can't always be as nice as we would like. We've got to be cruel to be kind. That's the way it's got to be. We don't actually hate the patients, but they've got to know who's in charge. Once they get the better of you, you're lost and the whole thing collapses.'

Rick thinks that people outside should not criticize the way the hospital is run either – they haven't worked there and cannot possibly appreciate the problems involved in organizing a ward of forty or so mentally handicapped people, with varying degrees of handicap, physical disorder, and emotional disturbance that can manifest itself in overt aggression.

This is all very well, but it lays the foundation for an 'anything goes' attitude – 'it's the way you've got to do it.' – 'the only language they'll understand.' Thus the rough treatment of patients, the constant harassment, the humiliation, are all part of 'the only way to do it.'

'*I don't like exploiting patients. But sometimes you have to. To show them who's in charge. Showing them up in front of others is a good way. It puts the others on their guard and gives them a good laugh as well.'*

Rick has noticed that the lads are becoming a bit restless, a bit cheeky. '*Too clever for their own good.*' His solution is to pick on certain '*troublemakers*' and send them to bed at four o'clock without their evening meal. An example to others as well as to teach them a lesson. '*It keeps them in check for a while,*' says Rick.

Dennis, named as one of the ringleaders, is summarily dismissed to bed. Upstairs, holding on to his bunk for support, Dennis sobs his heart out. But he absolutely refuses to get undressed: he can't understand what he has done wrong and defies all attempts to get him into bed. Difficult to know with Dennis if he's having you on or not. But sending a 43-year-old man to bed without his evening meal is a bit of a bad joke.

*   *   *

I was put on another ward – Canary – for an hour. The guy working there, who had started the same day as I did, said: ' You've got to shout at these bastards or they don't take any notice of you. If you're quiet with them they take the piss out of you and make things difficult. They need shouting at and a bit of a pasting to keep

*them down, know what I mean? See that guy over there, he had a
go at me yesterday so I put one on him. Said he'd report me to Heath
(the Chief Nursing Officer) but they all say that, don't they? You've
got to defend yourself, be fair.'*

*He abuses everyone he can, to show me I'm on his villa and he
knows the score and they know him.*

*'See that guy? He takes a poke at other nurses here, but when
he sees me he runs a mile. He knows what's good for him, you see.
Can't stand that bastard over there. All he wants to do is to stare at
you. Can you credit that? Stupid bastard.'*

It is not possible to show much tolerance to potentially disruptive behaviour when the efficiency of a large organization
depends on the smooth running of all its parts. In this respect a
mental handicap hospital is no different from any other institution; in schools and prisons too, large numbers of people
(pupils and prisoners) are supervised by a much smaller number of
staff (teachers, warders). The nursing staff in the hospital are
always vigilant, trying to anticipate and forestall any disorder.
When the relationship of staff to patients is thus one of necessary
surveillance, it is all too easy to see hospital life in terms of the
'management' of patients.

Not that surveillance and control are the official aims of
nursing care. Nurses are told they should try to 'establish a bond
between patient and nurse',[6] 'become a substitute parent',[7] or
'help each patient develop his (her) own potential to the maximum'.[8] The emphasis on control in a hospital does not mean that
staff–patient relationships have to be only management relationships. Clearly many other kinds exist. Nor need all forms of
control by the staff over the patients be necessarily wrong: there
are obviously many instances where a patient's behaviour could
be detrimental to him or herself or to other patients. There is
plenty of scope, too, for argument about what exactly is in the
best interests of a patient, or, for that matter, of other patients or
staff.

The staff's need for control over patients does, however, make
it extremely difficult for more positive relationships to either
emerge or survive. It also makes it easier to justify all forms of

domination over patients, whether warranted by a particular event or not. In these circumstances, patient-*care* almost inevitably becomes patient-*control*, both in practice and in terms of how nurses view their work. 'Constant supervision, observation and habit training' is how a nurse in one of the newest and best equipped hospitals described her work.[9] The phrase sums up all the features of an objectifying relationship.

But, and this must be repeated, ward staff themselves are also subject to control of all kinds. And it is imposed by an administrative and medical hierarchy which they often feel to be out of touch with the realities of ward life.

Bruce had a long chat with the charge nurse, Rick. Rick reveals that when he was a student he had good intentions and ideals, he wanted to see things changed. But the further he got up the ladder, the greater the pressure on all sides to conform, to accept the previously unacceptable, to implement schemes and ideas he didn't have any faith in. Rick detests the administration, the 'intellectuals' who constitute it. He sees them as a joke not to be taken seriously: how can they possibly know what goes on in the wards, at grass-roots level? But he also views them as a potential threat since ultimately they control his job. He maintains that the hospital could be the best institution around for the mentally handicapped were it not for the administration. But he now has a wife and a family to support. He knows that if he kicks too hard against the pressures, the irrational decisions he has to implement, then he would eventually be considered a candidate for the chop.

Democracy is said to exist on the ward by virtue of (sometimes) weekly staff meetings at which (supposedly) anyone can say anything. However, the charge nurse only records those points he himself agrees with or puts forward. Bruce made a point at a staff meeting that he considered very important. The following day he read the official report of the meeting that 'they' will get to see, and his point had been omitted. So much for 'channels' and 'feedback'! The administration only deals with what goes on in the villa through official channels, the charge nurse reporting to the unit officer, etc. This lack of direct feedback and the long chain of intermediaries works against the ward staff who feel hamstrung by procedures and red tape. There is a six-monthly sounding-off board, but that's as far as it goes. Many of the nurses are too afraid to show their feelings anyway.

As nurses in another hospital said: 'You only get a bad name if you keep fighting for things; you get labelled as a troublemaker. So you keep quiet in the end.'; 'I began to hate my job, knowing I shall never be able to change things.'[10]

Another significant way in which care becomes control is the frequent use of medical procedures to enforce order. 'We rely on tranquillizers rather than on organized activity to control the patients', is how a consultant in another hospital put it.[11]

At the first sign of trouble, out come the tranquillizers. A comment from Rick the charge nurse on why drugs are so prevalent as a means of treating the mentally handicapped: 'It saves us having to belt them when they go up the stick. If you belted Chris it might kill him. Or Colin or David, for that matter.'

Drugs are seen as the answer not to the patients' problems, but to the problem of keeping the villa peaceful and safe. Hyperactive and violent patients are dosed up for a bit of peace and quiet – no investigation is made into why they behave as they do. Those who frequently bite others are liable to have their teeth removed, not because their teeth are rotten or painful, but because their behaviour is a problem to others.

One study of ward medication in another hospital, carried out by a doctor, found that roughly half of all the patients concerned were on major or minor tranquillizers.[12] The nurses' reasons for requesting these and other drugs included swearing, 'excessive' masturbation, smearing faeces, being noisy, and various other kinds of behaviour, much of it very infrequent.

The behaviour cited as grounds for medication may well be disturbing and difficult for the nurses to tolerate, but tranquillizers are not necessarily the most therapeutic means of dealing with this. They are more appropriately used in the control of anxiety (on the part of the patient), or of schizophrenic or psychotic states. In the hospital studied, very little assessment was made of the effects of the drugs, or of any other way of altering the be-

haviour of patients. Drugs which might have had more therapeutic relevance to patients' needs, such as anti-depressants, were
scarcely used at all.

Care and control, treatment and discipline, are thus conflated.
Allegedly therapeutic drugs are used to enforce order. Order and
'good' behaviour are themselves seen as therapy for patients.
Thus the goals of treatment become transformed into conformity
to the demands of the institution. And the difficulties which
patients may experience in living in the highly controlled environment of the institution come to be seen as something which is
wrong with patients.

Lack of freedom is one of the least tolerable aspects of hospital
life, especially for more independent patients. Often the least of
activities – such as going for a walk – can be done only with the
explicit permission of a nurse. Any infringement of parole is
punished by loss of the privilege of being allowed out.

*Clive pissed off at ten o'clock one Sunday morning. The charge
nurse swore that he hadn't given him permission to go – the official
parole time is one o'clock. The charge was also looking after his
own skin. Clive returned, soaking wet but happy, at seven o'clock in
the evening. Bollocked instantly by the other charge nurse, while all
the time Clive insisted he had had permission to go.*

'As your punishment you won't be going to the dance tonight.'

*Clive's world crumbles, tears well up in his eyes, his happiness
shot to bits. When the charge goes off, a kind-hearted nurse lets
Clive go. Clive is very confused.*

That the staff's authority is unassailable comes across clearly
when hospital patients talk about their lives: 'If you speak your
mind, you're called cheeky. If you keep quiet, they tread on your
toes.'; 'It was terrible, you couldn't go out, you couldn't do this,
you couldn't walk about as you liked, had to stop in the ward.'[13]

Conflict between the desire for efficient management and the
demand that individuals be treated with a minimum of care and
respect is common to many large institutions. Goffman calls it a
conflict between treating people 'as means to an end' – as the raw
material of an organization that has to be run as smoothly as
possible – and treating them 'as ends in themselves' – discerning

and meeting personal needs.[14] Various studies have shown how detrimental an organization that is hierarchical and bureaucratic can be to personal contact. In a hospital the rigid adherence to hierarchy and job demarcation, plus the insistence on order and routine and a top-heavy administrative system, all ensure that running the institution takes priority over the individual needs of its inmates.[15]

This conflict of interests can seem obvious enough to an outside observer or to sociological analysis. But the staff do not necessarily experience their work in this way. It is remarkable that, in pressing for improved conditions, nursing organizations and journals seldom ask for structural changes in the organization of hospitals or for a different delegation of power and responsibility. They press mostly for more and better trained staff, higher pay, reduction in overcrowding, better buildings and facilities. Do they actually see themselves as caught in the trap between relating to the patients as humanly as possible and carrying out their work adequately according to the demands of the hospital bureaucracy? If not, what is their view of their work?

WORK

Nurse: '*All you've got to worry about in this job is if they get ill, or run away. Otherwise there's nothing to do.*'

'*If there's not any real nursing to do, this job is really boring. Nothing to do. I couldn't work on Sparrow, they're all high grade. They're all mobile and can feed themselves. There's nothing you can do for them. The time just drags. It's all so bloody boring, it'd drive me up the wall. No you wouldn't get me working there.*'

The fact that there are at least thirty patients to talk to, relate to, play with or enjoy – all this is boring. Making beds, clearing up shit, tidying lockers, now that's what work is. If it moves, change it, clean it, dress it, but don't bother to talk to it. What's the point? It's a waste of time.

* * *

The chief nursing officer sometimes takes himself off his backside and does a whistle-stop tour of the wards, unbeknown to anybody save himself. On one such lightning strike on Starling, he flashed past the kitchen and saw Bruce and myself talking to Simon. In typical hospital fashion, he didn't confront us with the question of what we were doing in the kitchen when we were supposed to be working. Instead he reported the 'incident' to a charge nurse, ordering him to delegate the responsibility for telling us off to the senior SEN. Nobody bothered to ask us why we were talking to Simon in the first place. Contrary to his accusation we were not 'loafing in the kitchen drinking tea,' but trying our utmost to get Simon to understand that if he carried on the way he was doing, life would be very arduous for him.

Mental handicap nursing in full and glorious colour! Make a bed and you get praised. Interact socially with a patient and you get accused of loafing. What a lot of the lads need is someone to talk to, get things off their chest, just talk. If the only people available think this is a waste of time, then not much good will ever come of this 'staff–patient relationship'.

* * *

Bruce moved to another villa, Canary, supposedly as a punishment for having two days more holiday than he was entitled to, a misunderstanding. This callous move meant that six months of hard work in building up relationships went down the drain, maybe for ever. Bruce cried that evening on his way home. Things had been starting to work out on the ward. Then this. That's how the place got to you. That's the effect the lads had on you. The hierarchical structure is to blame – decisions taken on bits of paper with names and numbers, no consideration given to the misery caused. What is worse, there is no appeal to these irrational decisions, not even an appeal to reason. A decision is taken in a vacuum and adhered to, no matter what the cost to both patient and staff, when ten minutes' discussion could prevent this.

Chris is completely up the stick, locked in a side room. I tried to reason with him. It worked to a certain extent.

'I want to see Bruce, Frank. I haven't seen him for a long time. Feel a lot better if I could talk to him.'

I went across to find Bruce on Canary but they wouldn't allow him to come back over. I consulted Rick, who was of the opinion *that since Bruce had left Starling, he had cut himself off from any contact – that was official. So Chris never got to see Bruce; he went right up the stick and got the needle for his trouble. Inflexibility, officialdom, red tape, blind following of official policy – tell Chris that, will he understand? I don't and I can't see that Chris should, either.*

A question was put to the chairman of the training school as to why the staff were shifted from villa to villa, often without reason.

'I don't think we do that. We wouldn't do that willy-nilly. Anyway if you are shifted, it's normally within the same unit, just another villa.'

'But even if that's true, we still lose contact with patients on the original ward.'

'When you are employed to work here, it isn't just for one ward. You have to go where you are needed.'

'Then what's the point of building up any form of personal relationship with a patient if you are going to be moved without warning? You might be at a critical stage in communicating with a particular patient, then suddenly it's cut off. What's the point?'

'It gives you experience on different wards. Anyway, take a ward like Starling, the new staff go there to get used to the place. When we consider them suitable to be moved on to a more difficult ward we shift them at that time.'

As a contrast, the same individual on another occasion: 'The reason we are here is building up personal relationships with the patients, creating a bond between patient and nurse.'

If only he would admit some of the anomalies of the situation, that all is not as it should be, instead of blindly defending hospital policy even when it contradicts itself. This lack of honesty permeates the system. Questioning what happens is dismissed as a waste of time – things will never change, it's always been this way.

So what does count as 'real' work? Either physical care of patients – keeping them clean and fed; or physical care of the ward – keeping it clean and tidy. Spending time with patients in other ways is not considered so important. Staff who do this get little support from others; they may even be seen as disrupting the smooth running of the ward.

If this is how staff define important work, it is not, primarily, due to their own short-comings but to the methods of organizing work within the hospital.[16] Both qualified and unqualified staff have to spend a large amount of their time on domestic work and on maintaining minimum physical care of the patients. One nurse described this work as 'body servicing': getting patients up, seeing that they are dressed, shaved, washed, toileted, fed, cleaned up, changed – all repeated several times a day. At the same time the ward has to be kept clean and tidy, beds made, clothes sorted.

Such work is done at particular points in the day, centring upon meal times; there are slacker periods in between, when many patients are off the ward. It forms not only the dominating context but also most of the content of the staff's relationships with patients. Routine is of prime importance in getting it done.

Every day of the year the lads get up at seven o'clock in the morning. An official 'lie-in' is never given, not even Sundays, Christmas or Easter, never. Everyone must be dressed for breakfast, no one can ever eat in their pyjamas. Nor can anyone ever wash and shave after breakfast – it always has to be done before. This is so arranged to suit the shift system and fit in with meal times.

Imagine a 'normal' person at home being told that for the next thirty years he must get up at seven o'clock sharp every single day ... The prospect of a patient ever being allowed the privilege of staying in bed until eight or even nine o'clock and still getting his breakfast when he gets up is a remote dream. Arguments which are put forward for maintaining this rigidity focus on the sheer weight of numbers: 'It would create more work for the staff, far outweighing the benefits it would give to the patients.' 'It's always been done that way' is another justification.

Those nursing staff who do see their work in terms of this routine frequently take great pride in doing it as efficiently as possible. The centrality of routine in the staff's work and the patients' lives has several functions. 'Routine makes for a smooth-running ward, minimizes disturbed behaviour, provides automatic checks that necessary procedures have been carried out for all patients, and prevents and lessens the effects of incidents.'[17]

Routine is also a way of coping with the high turnover of staff. It ensures that new staff can fit in easily, and carry out basic care with the least disruption: all that they have to do is learn the routine rather than what each individual patient is like. Since staff are expected to move easily from ward to ward, experience of doing this is part of what is valued in a good nurse.

That hospitals on the whole do not seem much concerned about these problems is borne out by the findings of a recent study of ward organization:

At the present time nurses and other specialists adopt a *laissez-faire* attitude towards the relationships of the mentally handicapped in their charge. They recognize that the mentally handicapped have relationships (e.g. with their relatives, with other patients, even with members of the staff) but they do not see it as their job to maintain these relationships . . . Furthermore, the figures for the movement of nursing staff suggest that they are not treated by the nursing administrators as an important source of relationships, and nurses' attitudes towards movement between wards suggest that at the moment they accept this view.[18]

Certainly there are very few suggestions from nurses themselves about how ward life and the distribution of staff could be reorganized to ensure more individual care and more consistent relationships for the patients. And this is despite the fact that other studies have shown that different methods of organization are feasible.[19] By lessening the degree of central control over wards or living units in favour of greater autonomy for the staff, and by lessening the reliance on a shift system, more flexible and individual care becomes possible, with a lower turnover of staff. Hospital training policies could also be changed so that student nurses spent much longer on fewer wards.

The emphasis on routine physical care of patients, and on domestic work, causes further problems for the staff. Most of the ward work does not require any specific nursing skill or medical knowledge. It does of course require other qualities such as patience, sensitivity and endurance. Knowledge acquired in training is thus only occasionally relevant to the direct care of a patient and usually only to those with specifically medical needs.

Many staff do actually feel that their training is largely unrelated to the requirements of daily life on the ward, and lay much more stress on experience and common-sense.[20] The low morale of many staff can be partly accounted for by having to do so much routine work that does not use their nursing skills – a lowering of their professional status.[21]

The non-technical nature of the routine work is especially problematic for more ambitious staff, those who want to make a career for themselves as nurses within the hospital structure. Such staff tend not to see basic care as real nursing, valuing instead medical activities such as taking blood-pressure and giving injections.[22] Frank observes in his diary that staff were exceptionally considerate when any of the patients became physically sick – a chance for them to demonstrate their 'real' nursing skills, to do what they have been trained to do. Physical sickness offers a possibility of cure or recovery – a possibility not usually present. This confusion about role may also contribute to the readiness to recommend psychotropic drugs, whatever their effectiveness – at least some medical treatment is being given and if it does not work, then it is the failure of the drug rather than of the nurses.

The hierarchical structure of the hospital also means that the more efficient and qualified the staff, the less time they spend with the patients. Indeed, one of the benefits of promotion, along with better pay and conditions and increased status, is the lessening of contact with patients and daily life on the ward. Success at work means moving *away* from patients rather than *towards* them – the ostensible reason for being there in the first place.

Nurses often claim that if hospitals were better staffed and had better facilities and resources, they would be able to give patients more individual attention. There is an inescapable truth in this, but it is over-simplifying matters to assume that life for the patients would automatically improve if staff numbers increased. Relationships can be distant and harsh even with more favourable staffing ratios. Institutional and personal barriers between people, stemming as they do from the way the hospital is organized, can remain whatever the numbers of staff. Extra staff, provided specifically to relate to patients, can become absorbed in the routine domestic activity of the ward.[23] It is also an over-simplification to assume that a more 'homely' atmosphere can be created by providing more domestic furnishings, or by minor architectural changes, as some official documents imply. Such inadequacies are an important part of the problem, but they do not alone explain what does and doesn't go on between staff and patients.

Many staff simply do not want, or are not able, to relate to patients in any other than a routine and distanced way. Slack periods, when the majority of the ward is out, are often not used to spend more time with the remaining patients.[24] Instead they are left to their own devices, with the staff taking a break for themselves, or else doing work that takes them away from the patients. Even in those periods when the staff are in close contact with the patients, they tend to be working *on* them rather than *with* them. Care-taking tasks, such as dressing and shaving, are often done in silence, or talking to other nurses. The opportunity to initiate any other kind of contact – playing or learning – is seldom taken. Shouted orders are sometimes the main form of verbal communication. Physical affection tends to be given very much in passing. Many staff feel it is dangerous for them to get 'too involved' with the patients. What is the reason for this holding back?

DISGUST AND DISTASTE

Another villa, Wren, makes Starling seem like paradise. Another world. Hardly a sound. Whole place reeks of piss and shit. None of the patients had any language or any control over their bodily functions, many were hyperactive. Yet they were constantly being cajoled into sitting stock-still in a particular chair. Nurses hardly talked to the patients, except for 'Sit down, shut up.' The charge wasn't bothered how the patients were dressed as long as they had shirts and trousers – that was enough. No consideration was given to the lads as human beings – bread was flung at them landing in pools of spilt tea as if they were the lowest form of life. Sauce was spread all over the food – no attempt was made to find out if the patients wanted it or not.

Only occasionally, however, do staff express their disgust at the patients.

'Dribbling, can't stand that dribbling, makes me sick. All that filthy dribble, all over your hands and down your clothes. Horrible, that's what it is.'

'They're like cattle, aren't they?' *'They look like a bunch of fucking monkeys, don't they?'*

Comparisons with non-human forms of life are common. Staff in one hospital classified the patients into three main categories: 'vegetating' for the cot-and-chair patients; 'animal' for the low grade but mobile ones; 'child-like' for the higher grade ones.[25] As a nurse in one hospital said: 'I've always felt that what they needed here was a vet, not a psychiatrist.'[26]

The problems facing the staff are put with an unusual directness by a nurse in another hospital:

Although staff have a degree of familiarity with patients as people, nonetheless there are certain activities that these handicapped children and adults take up that are always going to be regarded as animal – defecating; pissing; throwing down food at meal times; ripping clothes; rocking. Which is not so much animal as unnerving . . . there's a gut response . . . a definite drive to stamp out such behaviour which leads to a uniformity of response . . . and this is where you run into the effacing of personality and the unacceptable face of the institution.[27]

The profound effect that such behaviour can have on others is seldom acknowledged.

Andy, the villa's arch bully, genuinely afraid of the patients actually coming into contact with him physically.

'They're all fucking queer, this lot. Get away, you dirty bastard.' *Perhaps he thinks it's catching.*

Kath looks aghast that I have made the staff tea in one of the tea-pots used by the patients. She was nearly sick at the thought that tea would pass her lips that had even a remote connection with the patients. Clive received a right bollocking from Kath for giving her precious 17p mug to Eric to drink from in mistake for the correct, almost identical, one. Clive is bemused by the pettiness of it all

Kath feels she must now buy a new cup, as she is terrified she may catch some terrible disease if she comes into contact with the patients' cutlery or crockery. Yet every day she cajoles the patients into eating and drinking. Are we any different from the patients in our make-up?

Although expressions of disgust do slip out from some of the staff, this is neither an openly recognized part of the situation, nor does it happen in any way that could help nurses deal with these feelings. It is officially taboo that nurses could have such feelings towards their charges, and yet it is clear that they do, as would most people.

Tyne is one of the few researchers to write about the more distasteful aspects of mental handicap nursing.[28] In his study, incontinence was the main factor cited by staff as distinguishing mental subnormality nursing from other kinds of nursing, in spite of the many other factors they could have chosen – patients' communication problems or absence of cures, for example. At the same time, however, staff mostly professed unconcern about having to deal with incontinent patients. Some claimed they got completely used to it, becoming as they said 'immune'. Incontinence was never the subject of joking on the ward, although the patients themselves often were. The formal terms 'faeces' and 'urine' were always used, never 'shit' or 'piss' – one way of maintaining a professional distance. Although incontinence was frequently mentioned as one of the main features of the work it in fact received very little skilled or professional attention on the ward under study. Patients were segregated according to their degree of incontinence for management reasons, but most of the work involved cleaning up after the event, rather than anticipating it, or helping the patients deal with it themselves, or develop greater self-control. For the most part incontinence was regarded as unchangeable, an assumption that has been disproved by training programmes in some hospitals.[29]

The disgust patients arouse in other people is often increased by the degrading conditions in which they are forced to live. Toilets without doors, poor quality and often dirty clothing, shared toothbrushes, face-flannels and towels are common in many hospitals.

The conditions in one hospital where the superintendent had been suspended were recently described '. . . as if Dickens had come alive again in the 1970s in the middle of Teddington . . . a dirty hospital, with filthy wards, patient areas and domestic areas . . . the patients were dirty, smelly and with a bad state of dental care . . . they were poorly dressed in an undignified manner . . . and the hospital was short of clothes, particularly for children.'[30] And multiply handicapped children in several other hospitals were reported to be suffering from conditions of 'nineteenth-century poverty' – chronic catarrh, running ears, sore eyes, skin diseases, upset stomachs, bad teeth and worms.[31] Such conditions seldom come to light except as a result of public inquiries or research studies. We have seen how difficult nurses find it to complain, even about conditions that make it so hard for them to maintain reasonable standards of hygiene. What is more disturbing is that visiting specialists, paramedical staff, GPs or social workers, who must be well aware of these conditions, do not complain either.

The official failure to recognize these feelings of disgust or despair is not in the best interests of the patients, although it may superficially seem to be good nursing. The difficulties that nurses have in being in the continual presence of very handicapped people are simply not considered. Instead these problems are shelved, only to manifest themselves in the expressions of disgust and sadism that do slip out, and in the myriad of ways in which staff distance themselves. The structure of the hospital and the organization of work within it embody and justify the personal needs that staff have to maintain their immunity from the patients.

DISTANCE

The most visible sign of distance is the wearing of uniform and the importance attached to it.

At the ward meeting an official directive was read out from the Nursing Officer ordering all male staff to wear dark suits, white shirts, dark ties and a white coat at all times. The female staff were ordered to wear skirts, never trousers.

Rick attempted to justify the directive, aiming his comments directly at me.

'*I like all my staff to wear a white coat. It's much nicer and the big nobs like to see them. If the staff look scruffy the lads will only copy them. The lads like wearing suits and ties. The staff should wear the same. You can't do the job properly looking scruffy. Dressed as nurses, act as nurses.*'

Other staff comments after the meeting:

'*Uniforms exist as security for the patients. A sense of comfort and safety.*' *Is this the way the patients think? Do they feel insecure on outings when staff don't wear uniform?*

'*Sometimes if the patients look really smart you can't tell them from staff.*'

'*What's wrong with that, isn't it a good thing?*'

'*Of course not, visitors, or the fire brigade or other staff wouldn't be able to pick out a nurse if there's any trouble, an emergency.*'

'*I talked to this guy in the grounds for at least five minutes before I realized he was a patient, not a staff. Now if he was wearing a white coat I would have known right away. It would have saved a lot of time. You've got to be able to tell the staff from the patients, you might say something to the patient you wouldn't want them to hear.*' *Such as what?*

Instead of welcoming the possibility of confusion as a sign of the potential normality of the patients, the staff see it as a breaking down of the desirable order. As a patient in another hospital said: 'It's like the army, you see, the staff are in charge, that's why they wear uniform.'[32]

Distance between staff and patients is also marked by the fact that they do not eat together. Indeed staff are forbidden to, allegedly to prevent the stealing of patients' food. Eating together would provide many opportunities for learning basic social skills, as well as being a way in which hospital life could be made more normal at no extra cost. The hospital is not of course unusual in its separation of patients and staff for eating, although many residential homes and hostels do encourage staff to eat with residents when they are on duty. In almost all other hierarchical organizations different classes of people eat separately – workers and management in factories, students and teachers in universities, for example.

Frequent reference to the patients as 'them' or 'this lot' also reduces each person's individuality.

'No one is special.' Scrupulous fairness was to Kath far more important than individual satisfaction. She attempts to be fair to everyone in a perfect way, resulting in gross injustice to all. Individual requests for attention, access to a room or wardrobe, are squashed with remarks like 'Who do you think you are?'; 'This place isn't run for you.'; 'We can't spare one staff just for you.'

The only equality achieved by these attitudes is an equality of deprivation, largely forced on the staff by their scarce numbers and resources. However this denial of difference between patients, the grouping of them together as 'this lot', makes it even less likely that the staff will in any way identify with the patients. The most extreme form of this is seen in occasional remarks like 'It's all the same to them', and 'They've no feelings anyway.'

Simon for two days had not eaten or drunk anything, nor said a word to anybody. He had not been to work; he will get no money. He knows this. We know this. But nothing said to Simon makes any difference. He now has to be fed and is reverting to behaviour that he displayed a year ago.

Kath: 'Simon's a typical schizophrenic. Mr Williams said so. Either that or he's going through this queer behaviour as a result of his epilepsy.'

'Perhaps he's worried about something.' Another nurse, Sarah, gave me an incredulous look.

'What on earth can he have to worry about? He's got nothing to worry about. All his clothes are given him, all his food is free, he has a bed to sleep in. He should think himself lucky. Other people are worse off than him. What is there to worry him?'

'Don't you worry about things, Sarah? Don't things get you down?'

'Of course they do. But I'm normal, that's different. Not like these idiots. They haven't the brain to worry.'

'So we are not in any way like these lads?'

'*No, of course not, else they wouldn't be here, would they?*'

'*Why do you work here?*'

'*For money, of course.*'

'*And don't you have any feeling towards the lads except a fear of people like Tony?*'

'*Oh, I don't mind some of them, even Tony's not bad when he's not up the stick. But some of them are not very nice, are they? I mean they are not really human some of them, behaving the way they do. I mean any normal person would get a good belting if they carried on like these lads.*'

'*I'd rather go out for a meal in the evening with some of these lads than with some of the staff in this place.*'

'*You're fucking mad. You should be in here with the rest of these nutters.*'

The common division of people in general into either 'normal' or 'abnormal' sanctions the differences that are created between staff and patients within the hospital. Despite all avowals to the contrary by psychologists, the categories of normal and abnormal are seen as representing differences of kind rather than of degree. For example, two-thirds of the staff interviewed in one hospital thought that there was a sharp dividing line between 'normal' and 'mentally subnormal', despite being taught that there is a continuum.[33] It would seem that the people in closest contact with the mentally handicapped have the greatest need to mark the differences between them and their charges, to affirm their own 'normality' in the face of the perceived abnormality of their charges. The organization of the hospital helps them do this, at every point.

All of us, staff and otherwise, have complex reactions when confronted with handicapped people. They arouse in us fears of our own possible abnormalities and dependencies. What if I were like that? How would I feel about myself? Would anyone like me? Recognizing any similarity with handicapped people is very hard, because the enormous fear of being at all like that brings instantly to mind all the ways that we are not like that – they *are* different, there is no danger of being remotely like them. One of the most urgent tasks in the whole field of mental handicap is to help staff, whether inside or outside hospitals, to recognize and understand the fears aroused in them by mentally handicapped people. Acknowledging such feelings means that they can be put to one side rather than projected on to the recipients of 'care'.

The issue of the possible similarity between patients and staff, the recognition of what they have in common, is not a closed one, even within the hospital. The patients themselves assert their own humanity, make claims upon the emotions of the staff. They can be affectionate, humorous, upset, etc. in ways that make the staff respond as they would to anyone else.

Many hospital staff deliberately choose to enter this kind of work because they want to deal with people rather than with machines or commodities. Many of them struggle to maintain this sense of their work, despite all the pressures that separate them from the patients as human beings. Yet given that the hospital system does tend to make them simply into managers of the institution's 'raw material', is it surprising that so many either leave disheartened or else are forced to abandon their idealism?

Chapter 4

The Outside World

A hospital is a self-contained and segregated community. Even so, people visit the wards, staff have lives outside, and the patients themselves go out on trips, walks, visits home, or occasionally to work. Interaction between inside and outside is never easy. Visitors, including parents, are marginal to the hospital, in no way part of its life; while patients, when they go outside the hospital, often seem odd and institutionalized, unfamiliar with the conventions of ordinary life. Such confrontations, artificial and strained as they often are, expose the crucial issue of normality – the patients' difference from other people. The tension about this is contained in the enclosed world of the hospital, and by the clearly demarcated roles within it. But this tension surfaces in other situations which are more open and more ambiguous.

VISITORS

Every time someone of importance visits the villa the whole place gets turned upside-down, everyone is as nice as pie to the lads, everything as hunky-dory as circumstances and the hospital budget allow. June (a nursing assistant) says the only reason as she sees it for making the villa and the lads presentable is 'if any big nobs come round to see this place'. In an ordinary hospital, doctors come round all the time, but not here.

Canary, the supreme shit ward, was spruced up when the news broke that the Hospital Area Committee were due for a visit. The nurses did a great cover-up job, were nice to the patients, the charge nurse answering the committee's questions with considerable competence. One of the committee even put herself out to have a word with Bruce but never in a thousand years considered talking to any of the 'subnormals'. As do most visitors, they went away thinking what a grand job the hospital was doing and how humanitarian the nurses were.

To visiting relatives, however, the staff's attitude is very different.

Many of the nurses wish the parents had nothing to do with the lads.

'*It only upsets them. They've deserted them by sending them here, so why bother to visit them,*' Kath said.

'*You should've seen it. Terry's mum comes tramping across. Followed by Neil's mum. Then Sammy's. They were all there by a quarter past one.*'

'*Fucking cheek. If it'd been me, I'd have had them waiting until two o'clock. That's the time they're supposed to come and visit their precious little buggers. Fucking liberties these mothers take. They really get on your nerves. Her and her little Sammy. She sat next to me on the trip to the zoo and all she talked about was her precious Sammy. "Are you a nurse? Good, well you make sure he eats his breakfast, dinner and tea like a good boy." Makes you laugh, doesn't it? I'll give her her little Sammy, stuff him straight up her arse.*'

*   *   *

A very quiet, sad old lady knocks at the door of the villa. She has come to see her little Sammy (43 years old). She waits at least five minutes before the door is opened. She is led to a locked room where Sammy has worked himself into a frenzy over this visit. The door is unlocked, the two embrace. Sammy is told 'Mummy can't stay very long as she has to go somewhere.' A week's waiting, hours in a locked room, compulsory suit and tie in a heat-wave and then to be told his precious visitor can't stay very long. Because he can't put into words what he is feeling doesn't mean he feels any the less about what happens to him. Outwardly Sammy stoops a bit lower, sulks, becomes more aggressive.

*   *   *

In the vast majority of cases a visit by a parent or relative was well known in advance by both patients and staff. The visiting day was normally Sunday. Those who did get visited would spend the whole of Saturday and Sunday morning fretting, worrying, getting over-excited at the prospect of a two-hour visit, being threatened with all manner of nasty things if they dared get their best clothes dirty. For the likes of Roy, who has been getting into his best clothes every Sunday for years on end to await a visit which never has, and never will, come, these set visiting hours are hardly a good thing.

A fixed visiting time works for the staff and for the supposedly good name of the hospital. If the staff know exactly when the visits are to be made, then the patients to be visited can be got ready in clothes that are changed directly the visit is over. If visits are scheduled then the staff need only be 'nice' to the patients when a visit is in progress. A situation is thus set up where the staff resent the parents if they make unscheduled visits, or whose rare scheduled visit comes not on a Sunday – 'We don't get a chance to get them ready.'

There was talk in a ward meeting of allowing visiting hours every day at any time; but the general attitude was a wish that the parents would stay away altogether. 'They only upset what we are trying to do, they only see them once a week or less.'

We were told at a staff meeting not to tell the parents anything in case it harmed the good name of the hospital and upset the mothers at the same time. We were always to give the impression that everything was fine. 'Never deal with a visitor's inquiry yourself, you haven't the information available or the authority.' Possibly then it is only to protect their good name that the hospitals have set visiting hours, in case they ever get caught with their trousers down.

* * *

Simon was discussed at a case conference, because of his huge steps backwards with regard to everything over the previous weeks. It was suggested that a special conference be set up specifically for Simon's case and that his parents be invited to attend. Rick dislikes the involvement of parents, especially where the patient's treatment is concerned. He feels that their presence would hamper the dis-

cussion – presumably with the parents present certain facts would be omitted or distorted 'in order to protect everybody concerned'. Rick feels that the parents don't really understand their children as they see so little of them, so how can they be of any use at a case conference? The psychologist tries eloquently to defend the parents but fails to convince Rick. He even admitted that he was a little apprehensive of discussing the patients with their parents – and he's supposed to be the expert on human behaviour. He puts that burden firmly on the shoulders of the social workers.

Most patients have very few visits. Surveys have found that about one-third of all patients in mental handicap hospitals are *never* visited, within one year.[1] Only one-quarter are visited more than once a month. Even fewer patients leave hospital to visit their families; three-quarters never do so. Other studies confirm this lack of family contact. Many patients are too old to have parents who are still alive or able to visit. Hospitals are often remote and difficult to reach by public transport. Also, visiting is less frequent in the large hospitals, compared to the more local small ones, or hostels.

Hospitals can also make it difficult for relatives to visit or feel that their visits have been worthwhile. Official policy in many hospitals may be to welcome visitors at any time; but in practice visiting is usually confined to certain days and hours. Such restrictions can be reinforced by staff's behaviour towards visitors; only offering tea, for example, on what they regard as visiting days. Relatives often have to ask for permission for and give advance notice of visits; they are even liable to be told that they come too often.[2]

The staff's inaccessibility to parents has often been commented on. Senior staff or doctors can only be seen by appointment. In some cases, parents have not seen a doctor since their child was first admitted and are unable to find anyone to talk to who knows about their child's condition.[3] In others, parents are too intimidated to even ask the simplest facts about their child's life – how well he or she has been eating, for example, or why he or she has been transferred to another ward.[4]

It is not easy to become an occasional visitor to someone whose daily life you were once central to. If non-verbal care-taking has been the main focus of the relationship, this difficulty is especially acute. Most parents are anxious about whether their child is being adequately looked after and is happy; these worries are often met with bland reassurance or with resentment. Parents also have to cope with all their own feelings of loss at separating from someone they have looked after for years. They are bound to find it difficult to establish a new relationship with their child and the hospital does not give them much support in trying to do so.

It is not surprising that some relatives give up; what is more surprising is that many persist. A few hospitals do encourage and support parents – parents can help in the daily life of the ward, for instance, and continue to care for their own child.[5] Such hospitals report much more frequent visiting than others.

Visits can, of course, be difficult for the staff – it is they who often have to cope with an upset patient after a relative has left. They may also feel that parents are unduly critical of them. Doctors, as well as nurses, can be very dismissive of parents' needs. One pilot scheme, set up to improve communication between providers and users of health services, found doctors totally unwilling to co-operate, maintaining not only that existing channels of communication were adequate but that parents often didn't listen anyhow![6] The parents for their part said that they received very little of the information they needed from doctors and that doctors were frequently unwilling to admit they didn't know the answers to parents' questions. This was also found in other studies.[7]

A widely used textbook for nurses echoes this dismissive view of parents.[8] Readers are warned that parents may be 'over-anxious' about their child's welfare and have difficulty accepting a 'reasoned' explanation from the staff about their child's condition. Parents are seen as irrational, nurses as reasonable. Anger or criticism on the part of parents is allegedly their own guilt, projected as blame on to the hospital staff.

It is, in fact, a very widespread assumption among professionals that parents of mentally handicapped people feel very guilty, both for having given birth to a handicapped person, and for ceasing to look after their child in their own homes. Yet parents' accounts of their own experience do not always support this.[9] Frustration and despair are just as common. The possibility that parents may have something very real to complain about – namely the conditions of life they and their children are forced to endure – is never considered in the professional literature. Parents often have no alternative but to accept what meagre services are available. The state of relationships between nurses and parents in one hospital was described as follows:

> We find that parents who are critical of the way their children are cared for are resented by many of the nursing staff and indeed by some of the medical staff. The attitude is prevalent, 'If they can't manage their child themselves, why criticize us when we have so many more to care for?' This has on occasions led to nurses saying, 'If you don't like it, you can always take him home.'[10]

It is hardly helpful for nurses to be told that most of the problems in relationships with parents lie in the alleged psychopathology of parents. Recognition is needed for the very real difficulties involved, which stem from the respective roles of both parties, determined as they are by the conditions of life in the hospital. More emphasis is certainly needed on the positive aspects of continued parental involvement, since there is ample evidence that this is what parents want.

It is perhaps difficult to understand why nurses see relatives as such a threat to themselves. Why can they not welcome parents as helping them in their work, as alleviating the bleakness and the pressures of ward life? Interruption to routine is one important factor. Since staff have no official authority over relatives, any interruption from them would seem to threaten their sense of control and efficiency. Greater integration of visitors into ward life would require a different organization of work and responsibility, a more flexible system of care.

Parents are also less gullible than official visitors or distant administrators; thus they are more likely to expose any discrepancy between the public image of ward life and the reality. They are more liable to notice cuts, bruises or neglect, or to criticize the nurses. Unlike hospital officials, they do not have the 'good name' of the hospital to defend. Nevertheless, parents are often in too weak a position to voice complaints effectively, since they too are dependent on the staff who look after their child and may fear that he or she will be scapegoated if they make too much 'trouble'.

Relatives by their very presence also remind staff that patients (those who are visited) are real people, the objects of love and concern to other people in the outside world. Parents bring patients to life as the child of a mother or father who is much like anyone else. Relatives and friends, special to each patient, undermine the staff's perception of patients as completely 'other', a mere undifferentiated 'lot'.

Parents also confront the staff with the possibility that they should be behaving differently towards their charges – more like actual parents. One of the official roles prescribed for nurses is after all that of substitute parent, although by no means all staff see their work in this light. In one hospital it was found that it was mostly those staff who had *least* ambition to advance up the hospital hierarchy who did.[11] They were also the ones who spent most time with the patients. Even for these staff, however, providing 'parental' care did not necessarily mean sustaining long-term relationships so much as showing affection towards the patients by hugging and kissing them, or bringing them small presents. And even these attentions tended to be irregular and random, depending on all the other demands made on the staff. Adopting a parental role can also mean seeing the patients as children, whatever their age, assuming the right to total authority over them and dispensing immediate physical punishment if they do anything wrong.

For nurses who do see themselves as substitute parents, the real parents or other relatives are likely to evoke feelings of competition, as well as accentuating the deficiencies of the substitute parent. These deficiencies may well be the result of overall conditions of life in the hospital rather than the fault of individual staff, but they exist nonetheless. On the other hand, those nurses who do not see themselves in this way are likely to see parents as a threat in that they turn 'them' into 'something special' and thus undermine the staff's professional objectivity. In all this neither the patients' nor the parents' needs gain much expression and the importance of each to the other is neither publicly acknowledged nor validated. What becomes paramount instead are the needs of the institution and the needs of the staff as created by their professional roles within the institution.

OUTINGS

If visitors create problems for the hospitals, what difficulties occur when patients visit the outside world?

I was asked to take a few of the lads down to the village for a walk. As this was the first time I had been 'out' with the lads I felt a little apprehensive, not for myself, but for the lads if the public reaction was what I imagined. At this hospital outings and trips, even into the village, have really only got going in the past few years, so perhaps the locals need time to adjust. Kids either run away in mock fear, or openly deride and take the piss out of the lads. Young children are ushered away. Cold stares of fear and ignorance are directed at innocent faces. Often they are patronizing which can be worse than open hostility. Their faces often betray their feelings. All because they are face to face with someone who looks not quite as they should, walks slightly differently, maybe talks unintelligibly. Some of the lads love addressing people they meet; they wave, offer their hands. This friendliness is not always returned.

The hospital training these lads receive is so antipathetic to a normal way of life as to be permanently damaging and detrimental to any attempt to introduce a patient into the 'community', especially if the patient has been receiving such training for fifteen or twenty years. Getting these lads to walk together down the street instead of in Indian file, one behind the other, is a full-time job.

I took the lads over to see a football match being played in the hospital grounds. 'Are they allowed to have cigarettes?' asked a rather nervous spectator, emphasizing the apparent dichotomy between normal and subnormal beings – similar to the zoo syndrome 'Do not feed the animals.'

*   *   *

A day out at Brighton. A day away from the villa. A day to remember. The lads were all ready by nine o'clock. We weren't scheduled to go until an hour later, by which time Sammy had got changed again, and was on his knees scrubbing the kitchen floor. Ed really into his 'fucking this, fucking that' mood at anybody near enough to hear. Eventually we all set off with money to spend. It was snowing. It was snowing even more at Southend, a blizzard. After a hectic time in the toilet (one of five mass waterings) we strolled along the sea front. The lads were great. Brian was chatting to everybody. Ed forgot to 'fuck this and that'.

Dinner was in a large promenade cafe. A very civilized occasion. The lads were, obviously, unaccustomed to being asked what they wanted to eat. Apart from Ed talking in an incredibly loud voice, and their insistence on stacking the plates, arranging the cutlery, and looking for the slop bucket, everything was fine. The owner of the place was very helpful, we didn't drive anyone out of the cafe and no harm was done. And why should there be?

We went on the pier, and into the amusement arcade, everybody had a bit of a laugh. Roll-a-ball in the alley went down a treat, and even Jack, who is often loath to do anything, got into it.

In all the big stores we went into, the escalators were the biggest attraction. In Woolies Sammy had all the staff around him as he tested their knowledge on the price of alarm clocks. The exclusive stamp shop will never be the same again – Sammy tripped up the step, the staff got more edgy every minute. Harry eventually chose his day's purchase. We all shuffled out of the shop, sighs of relief behind us. Startled the clientele in the pub at first, but it didn't last. Shandies and a Babycham, everyone was happy. Jack always asked permission to do anything, go to the toilet, smoke.

* * *

Ice show – Cinderella – parents came. Different atmosphere altogether, the staff were ever so nice to everybody, that was hard to take. The idea of such a trip has its limitations and disadvantages, but the lads enjoyed it. Do they feel the way they are stared at, scrutinized, so difficult to avoid with a large group?

Toilets a riot, at the end everyone in various stages of exposure and undress.

Highlight of the show – Chris describing one of the clown's actions: 'He's wanking, sir, look he's wanking.' Exactly my feelings too – that didn't go down well with the Derby and Joan club seated behind us. The attitude of the staff changed immediately once the parents left: 'I've been at this fucking work away from my family for fourteen hours, now fuck off before I smash you in the face.'

All the lads remembered of the pantomime was the dogs playing football in the interval.

*   *   *

One Saturday afternoon Keith 'escaped' from the villa. The staff split up in their efforts to locate him. The weather was abysmal, the rain heavy and cold. I was given a brand new hospital-issue raincoat to wear, a variety which local people associate with the patients. By the time I reached the hospital gates, I looked extremely bedraggled, wet from top to toe, my normally speedy gait reduced to a laborious shuffle, to match the way I was feeling. Keith could be anywhere. I thought the local shops were a reasonable bet. I realized I was getting some extremely weird looks – after all what would you think if somebody peered through windows, entered shops, walked round and out again, looking at none of the merchandise, and seeming in a sorry state? Added to that you are wearing an identical coat to those 'nutters from up the road'. I was identified as a patient and it wasn't very pleasant. Shifty looks, children ushered away. Do the patients feel this rejection and sometimes instant hostility? It's a sorry state of affairs when the sight of a patient from a local hospital triggers off such a massive defence mechanism, so great as to prevent any kind of contact, even a hand proffered in friendship, 'in case the guy starts talking to me, or attacking me, or whatever', as one local person told me.

A lot of people are really great when it comes to making contact with the residents, but over all this built-in fear and ignorance of the handicapped is as great a hurdle to overcome as is the institutionalized behaviour of the residents considered for release.

On outings there is a double fear present all the time: one, that patients will misbehave, do something bizarre and upset the public; two, that this same public will be hostile and hurtful to the patients. The public is highly variable. Some people show great understanding and helpfulness, some excessive curiosity, others indifference, outright rudeness or fear. It can only be imagined – since no one has tried to find out – what patients themselves experience on outings. How does it feel to walk down a street, not knowing whether children are going to call you rude names, whether adults are going to give you curious looks, turn away, or smile protectively? What is it like to go into a shop not knowing whether the shop assistant will be helpful, disconcerted or impatient and to have the whole viability of making a purchase dependent on that?

Such unpredictable responses have little to do with how any single mentally handicapped person actually behaves on a particular occasion; they are determined more by the pre-existing attitudes of any members of the public they happen to come across. This makes mentally handicapped people peculiarly powerless, unsure of what they can and cannot influence in their immediate environment. Mentally handicapped people have been described by psychologists as outer-directed rather than inner-directed – relying, that is, on other people's suggestions and ideas far more than on their own resources and initiative. This is not so much a fault in them (as psychologists sometimes make out) as a feature which is central to the psychology of powerlessness – of having very little sense of the effect of one's actions on other people. It is also a response to a world which sees and treats mentally handicapped people as stereotypes, not individuals. The world is actually more confusing and less amenable to their control than for most non-handicapped people.

Outings also present a tense and delicate situation for the staff. As well as not knowing how the public will react, they do not know how their charges will behave in new circumstances either. Nor can they rely on using the usual institutional means of controlling them: shouting orders, for example, may be unremarkable on a ward, but unacceptable in public. Some staff may welcome outings as a chance to escape the confines of hospital, to have a spree and indulge the patients, but others find them difficult to manage, stressful and unrewarding.

ABNORMALITY AND NORMALITY

Outings reveal how very different the patients are from other people – they dress differently, walk around in a group or even in Indian file, stack the crockery in restaurants, shake hands with people they don't know. Out in public, the issue of normality, no longer hidden within the abnormality of the hospital, is unavoidable. The staff want their charges to be as unnoticeable and as ordinary as possible, yet they also know that whatever their efforts, some of the patients are going to seem strange to other people. In addition, the staff's roles and much of their sense of who they are in relation to the patients are based on the very fact of the patients' difference from other people. If the patients were more like normal people, then what would there be for the staff to do?

We have previously seen how the differences between staff and patients are reinforced and exaggerated inside the hospital. Goffman suggests in *Asylums* (Penguin, 1961) that a strong sense of the abnormality of the inmates may be necessary to the life of an institution, to preserve both its internal role system and its barriers to the outside world. This takes the form in subnormality hospitals of an exaggeration of the patients' incompetence and dependence. Frank records how disparaging some of the staff were about the likely effects of 'bungalow training' – a system of teaching more independent habits within the hospital grounds.

Staff tend to be very pessimistic about what can be done with lower grade patients.[12] In wards for multiply handicapped children, for example, their immediate aims were for the children to sit quietly in their wheel-chairs, to eat well, and to not be noisy, dirty or smelly.[13] Their longer-term aims were to fit patients into adult wards without any nuisance. Even with the more independent ones, they tend to emphasize how socially incompetent they are and often have extremely limited objectives for what they hope to achieve with their charges.[14]

Staff are often reluctant to accept the possibility of patients leaving hospital. Some of this reluctance is based on a real and justified scepticism about the adequacy of many community facilities. But there is also a reluctance to believe that patients' abilities and behaviour might be very different in a different environment.[15] This is one of the consequences of a medical approach to mentally handicapped people.

Pessimism can also manifest itself as lack of interest or hostility on the part of ward staff towards educational and therapeutic activities within the hospital. Resentment and lack of communication between the different departments are often reported. The bitterness with which nurses frequently express their scepticism about what 'therapy' can achieve is exacerbated by the fact that usually only the most promising patients are considered eligible for education or occupational therapy. The most difficult ones are left for the nurses to cope with on the wards. It is hardly surprising that many nurses find it difficult to accept the idea that they should have a more educative role towards their charges, as they are now constantly urged.

We can see that there is no transition, no easy flow, between life inside a hospital and life outside. This is as true for visitors and new patients coming into a hospital as it is for inmates leaving it, whether for brief outings, for visits home, or for the start of a new life. The more radical the departure from normal life within the hospital, the more difficult is any transition for all those concerned. As Goffman has shown, the sharp distinction which has to be preserved between life inside and life outside a total institution is one of its inherent features. Inmates are encouraged to perceive the institution as their total reality. In a subnormality hospital, the usual means of contact with the outside world – telephone, radio, letters, newspapers, etc. – are simply beyond the capacities of many patients. Visits and outings are their main means of alternative experience to the institution. Patients are almost entirely dependent on staff to encourage and organize these contacts. Staff, however, do not often show that much interest, let alone acknowledge the value of them.

Five lads came back after a two-week holiday. No one was interested in asking them where they had been, what they had done, whether they had enjoyed themselves, what they had bought. They might as well have been out for a ten-minute ride, carrying their suitcases to an imaginary holiday camp in the village, for all the interest it created. Within a few minutes they had been completely integrated back on the villa. The experience might just as well not have occurred.

If life within the hospital were less abnormal, more like life outside, would it not be easier for visitors and relatives to be integrated into the patients' daily lives? And easier for staff to train patients for a more independent life outside? The greater the gap between life inside and life outside, the more barriers have to be set up and the more unbridgeable the differences become between the handicapped people inside and the non-handicapped outside.

Even where the introduction of 'normality' is attempted, it tends to be in a bizarre or outmoded form, an exaggeration of certain social conventions. So the attempt described by Frank (page 37) to change the meals system resulted in a restaurant style of ordering food, not in anything more domestic. Often a rigidly conventional 'normality' is insisted on: haircuts are short and old-fashioned, formal suits are the men's best clothes, women never wear trousers, church services are obligatory except in exceptional cases and adult wards are sexually segregated. It sometimes seems that to be normal at all, mentally handicapped people have to learn to be supernormal.

If Kath upsets a food tray on the floor, she laughs it off with 'What a mess I've made.' If Clive does the same thing he's told what a 'fucking imbecile' he is. When a patient is given a chance to make it outside, perfection is demanded. If not, he is recalled to the hospital. In the bungalow training he is given marks out of ten for a tidy room, well-made bed, clean floor, etc. How many so-called normal people would be disqualified from a normal existence on such a scale? People outside don't always have a blue fit if wardrobes are untidy, beds unmade, cups of tea knocked over. Surely

*everyone, even the mentally handicapped, is entitled to make
mistakes.*

*Some of the lads spend hours on end twirling pieces of string and
gaining enormous pleasure from doing this. It is classified as 'self-
stimulating' behaviour and considered to be a characteristic of the
severely subnormal. The staff also twirl pieces of string. But this is
considered normal because there's a key on the end of it.*

The issue of normality is present in every interaction between
handicapped and non-handicapped people. And it is crucial to
both, although in different ways. Many normal people do not
know how to behave in the presence of a mentally handicapped
person. What after all do you do when someone, after a brief
introduction, behaves towards you as if they had known you all
their life, asking you intimate details about yourself? Or when
someone tells you, a well-meaning visitor in a hospital ward, that
they would like you to leave immediately? Or when someone
insists on shaking hands with you for half an hour?

Many mentally handicapped people, despite their anxiety to
appear as normal as possible, do flout minor social conventions.
They often express what others do not allow themselves to think
or feel. Some people find this refreshing, a welcome challenge to
the normal limits of everyday interaction and one of the rewards
of working with mentally handicapped people. Others find their
encounters with the mentally handicapped more uncomfortable.
They may stand at a distance and speak more loudly or slowly
than usual. They may become excessively jocular or excessively
protective.

Goffman described how some of the embarrassment between
the physically handicapped and normal people is dealt with by the
former underplaying their abnormality, emphasizing instead those
ways in which they are in fact normal.[16] A fiction of normality is
maintained. The need to deny difference arises as much from a
normal person's inability to cope with abnormality as from a
handicapped person's need to 'pass' as normal. Indeed the latter
need is often created by the former.

Mentally handicapped people do not have the same opportunity to co-operate with normal people in such denial of differ-

ence. They are probably neither able nor willing to help them deal with their discomfort. Although they may desire to be accepted as normal as much as other handicapped people do, their scope for appearing or being treated as normal is considerably less. Constrained by the all-encompassing nature of their handicap, they are all the more at the mercy of other people and their responses to it.

Chapter 5

The Historical Background

Historical accounts of mental handicap tend to be mainly concerned with institutional and legal landmarks – the building of an asylum, the passing of Acts of Parliament. Or they deal with the deeds of great men – scientific discoveries and educational reforms.[1] Recently, theoretical studies of the social history of madness, and of dependency and deviancy generally, have flourished, but similar studies of mental handicap have hardly begun.[2] Virtually nothing is known of the lives of idiots and their families. Mentally handicapped people are still as hidden from history as they are from the rest of life. What history they do have is not so much theirs as the history of others acting either on their behalf, or against them.

What particularly concerns us in this account is the way in which idiots have been seen at various points in history; how their differences from other people have been described and dealt with; what blame or stigma has been attached to them. Within this we will look at the origins of our present day hospitals.

It is usual to begin any history of mental handicap with the growth of scientific interest at the end of the eighteenth century, followed by the setting up of the first schools and asylums in the mid-nineteenth century. Everything before then tends to be seen as a blank and barbarous slate; everything since as progress, apart from the custodial period of the early twentieth century.[3] This not only misrepresents the past but also ignores the fact that we are still wrestling with many of the same problems that concerned people in the past. Are idiots truly human? What are the causes of their birth? How should they be treated? Such questions reflect the extent of the doubts about their full status as human beings, as much as they do any humanitarian concern about their welfare. The present day debate about the conduct and future of mental handicap hospitals is simply the modern form in which these questions emerge.

We are now witnessing an era of intended reform, a proliferation of new educational technologies and new forms of institutions for mentally handicapped people, as Chapter 6 describes. There is a similar sense of wanting to break with a dark past as there was in the mid-nineteenth century. Reform then turned rapidly into repression. This chapter looks at this transition and the subsequent developments that have left us with our present situations and attitudes.

EARLY WRITINGS

Before the late eighteenth century discussions of idiocy are scattered and fragmentary; those that do remain show clearly a preoccupation with the human status of idiots and with their origins. One of the more extended treatises is that of Paracelsus, a Swiss physician of the early sixteenth century. His account of fools is detailed and searching.[4] Wishing to establish the full humanity of fools, he proposes a fundamental Christian argument: '. . . his (man's) wisdom is nothing before God, but rather that all of us in our wisdom are like the fools . . . Therefore the fools, our brethren, stand before us . . . And he who redeemed the intelligent one, also redeemed the fool, as the fool, thus the intelligent one.' And further: '. . . death drives away from them the folly, the fantasy and so on, and it is the man within who perceives himself . . . even if the nature went wrong, yet nothing has been wrong with the soul and the spirit.' Paracelsus states that fools are not only equal to other people in God's eyes but even superior, being nearer to God. They differ from 'wise men' because the 'animal body they inhabit has been marred . . . the wisdom that is also in fools, like light in a fog, can shine through more clearly.' The wise man sometimes resists the 'true man' in his animal body, the fool does not. Just as God made prophets with a crazy 'animal body' so people should listen to fools, especially those not pushed around by other people. Instead of which, Paracelsus notes, people mostly scorn them because they lack both understanding and control of their reason. Paracelsus's idea that idiots do not suffer from as many worldly corruptions as others and are nearer to some truer or more basic conception of human nature persists into the present.

On the other hand, the notion that idiots are a consequence of the evils of mankind is also a recurrent theme in the Christian world. St Augustine states clearly that fools are a punishment for the fall of Adam and other sins.[5] Paracelsus does not blame individual parents for the birth of fools, as later writers did; for him, fools are simply one aspect of the way the whole of mankind has lost God's image. He favours kindly and respectful treatment of them, as an assertion of their rightful place in humanity.

What, however, causes wise parents to beget fools? Paracelsus maintains there is nothing defective in the material supplied by parents but something wrong in the subsequent processes that are beyond their control. Nature is a workshop inhabited by craftsmen, and children are made by carvers from the wood supplied by their parents. Fools are produced when inept apprentice carvers make mistakes and carve badly, as often happens. This picture has a similar logic to much later explanations of what was known as congenital idiocy, for example, the accounts of mongolism put forward before the discovery of chromosomal defects.[6] Combined accounts of fools, in terms both of their religious meaning and of defective causal mechanisms, were commonplace and continued to be so until the end of the nineteenth century.

It is not clear what the context of Paracelsus's treatise was, who he was arguing against, or whether any of his ideas were accepted. However, in the Middle Ages and before, there were many myths about changelings, children who were born deformed, handicapped or in some way peculiar: 'Fairies stole a mother's child from its cradle, and in its place laid a changeling with a big head and staring eyes who wanted to do nothing but eat and drink.'[7]

This is a story that has been embellished in all kinds of folklore and beliefs which have been handed down through centuries. Changelings were seen as sub-human, not born of a human mother. They came from the non-human underworld of envious demons, elves, fairies, etc. in exchange for the stolen human child. Their non-human status did not necessarily mean they were treated badly – indeed they were sometimes treated particularly well in the belief that this would ensure the good treatment of the stolen human child.

In these accounts, blame is attributed neither to the individual parents nor to mankind as a whole. All parents were exposed to the danger of having their child stolen even if they took every precaution. Blame and responsibility were directed outwards, on to the non-human underworld, beyond the control of ordinary people.

The Christian form of the idea of the handicapped child as an exchange can be seen in Luther's belief that it is the devil who has stolen the human child and then substituted himself for it. 'The devil sits in such changelings where the soul should have been.'[8] Changelings, 'more obnoxious than ten children with their crapping, eating and screaming', were just lumps of flesh with no soul; Luther even recommended killing them.[9] This is an early example of the common association of idiots with animality – no soul and over-dominant bodily functions – which was to become a familiar theme by the end of the nineteenth century.

The idea of handicapped children being a punishment for the sins of individual parents, rather than for those of mankind in general, is seen clearly in Luther. He explains the presence of abnormal children as stemming from the misdeeds of their parents – those who did not fear God enough, who bore illegitimate children, thought bad thoughts or cursed their offspring.[10]

The idea that abnormal children were the result of sexual intercourse between a woman and the devil was also common at the time. And for a long time giving birth to a handicapped child was grounds, in Europe, for considering a woman to be a witch. These are instances of blaming the mother specifically – a theme that was also to recur with much emphasis in the nineteenth and early twentieth centuries.

From the sixteenth century onwards there are scattered references to cretins.[11] These were particularly numerous in certain valleys of the Swiss Alps, due to deficiencies in the drinking water.

Their deformed appearance – they suffered from large goitres – and odd behaviour made them seem hardly human to astonished travellers and other observers. An account written in 1574 notes that '. . . many fatuous people are found . . . who hardly deserve to be named people, since they use no human food; . . . one who used horse-droppings, another one who used hay, others who walked naked the whole winter and various monstrosities of this sort.'[12] Their ugliness was sometimes grounds for considering them as only semi-human: 'They have a hardly human face, a large mouth and spittle flowing down.'[13]

Their appearance and behaviour also gave rise to spectres of sensuality and immorality: 'They are deaf, dumb, imbecile, almost insensitive to blows, and carry goitres hanging down to the waist; rather good people otherwise, they are incapable of ideas, and have only a sort of violent attraction for their wants. They abandon themselves to the pleasures of the senses of all kinds and their imbecility prevents them seeing any crime in this.'[14] The idea that idiots enjoyed their animal nature is yet another one which occurs again later. In the same account cretins were also seen as a separate sub-species of man, comparable to albino Negroes and other alleged curiosities – foreshadowing again the nineteenth century and its ethnic comparisons of idiots with so-called primitive people.

On the other hand the cretins, it seems, were regarded by the Swiss valley inhabitants themselves as angels from heaven, a blessing to their families and incapable of sin. A family without one regarded itself as being on bad terms with heaven.[15] They were well looked after, if contemporary accounts are to be believed, often with special hospices for their care. This super-human status accorded to Swiss cretins by the people they lived among is unique in European history. It contrasts especially strongly with the more negative sub-human descriptions of them given by outside observers.

We do not know even now what it was about the life of the valley inhabitants that allowed them to see their idiots so favourably. But it is clear that an understanding of the social basis of these attitudes is vitally important to any overall understanding of idiocy. It is possible that the obviously endemic and environmental nature of cretinism lessened the tendency to blame and stigmatize. Cretinism could have been perceived simply as an unalterable fact of nature, part of the divine order of the world, rather than of the misdeeds of mankind.

By the sixteenth century, too, the link between cretinism, goitre and the drinking water of certain valleys was known and discussed in contemporary medical literature. Cretinism shows a particularly close association between mental and physical abnormalities and it may have been this which influenced later writers to believe that all forms of idiocy had a definite organic basis. Idiocy in general has often been confused with cretinism: the name 'cretin' has sometimes been used to refer to all kinds of idiots and is occasionally used in everyday speech now.

The general assumption of the organic cause of idiocy was not much questioned before the twentieth century, when 'social' categories of defectives were devised. As cretinism is also such a clear example of the environmental causation of idiocy, it is interesting that, in contrast to the organic views, this knowledge does not appear to have modified subsequent theories on the hereditary basis of idiocy, nor to have encouraged much investigation of other possible environmental or endemic causes. This is but one example of the general bias in the whole field towards any kind of hereditary explanation.[16]

It was a seventeenth-century English physician, Willis, who was the first to propose what was later to become a very common view of degeneration. Trying to answer the question of how fools could be born to intelligent, as opposed to foolish parents, he supposed that, apart from accidents at birth, there was something defective in the material supplied by parents for reproduction.[17] Willis argued that the defects arose from their behaviour. Parents (to paraphrase Willis) might do too much studying and reading, causing them to be 'weakly prolific', too much energy being directed to the mind as opposed to the body. Or there may be 'somatic insults' to the bodies of parents through intemperance, drunkenness, effeminacy, luxury or excessive youth or age.

Willis also suggested that sometimes the size and texture of the brain was abnormal, apparently one of the earliest ideas about this. In seeing stupidity as sometimes the result of brain impairment, Willis likened it to other diseases which do not reduce the human character of the sufferer. Like Paracelsus, he also recognized that stupidity could not be cured, but he did emphasize the importance of both physicians and teachers in alleviating it.

One of the earliest appeals for some kind of public provision for idiots was made by Daniel Defoe at the end of the seventeenth century. It did not, however, materialize. He argued for the creation of a 'public fool house' to be paid for by a tax on learning, levied on the authors of books, on the grounds of a kind of natural justice.[18] At the same time he attempted to wrestle with the problem of how to fit 'born fools or naturals' into humanity. 'Perhaps,' he wrote, 'they are a particular Rent-Charge on the Great Family of Mankind left by the Maker of us all – like a younger Brother, who tho' the Estate be given from him, yet his Father expected the Heir should take some care of him.' Care should be taken of fools, said Defoe, as a tribute to God's bounty to mankind, a tribute to be paid to all those who lacked this bounty. Defoe also likened fools to animals, for the apparent 'deadness of their souls'.

Until more research is done, the above and other accounts will remain no more than disembodied fragments, unconnected to either the practice of the authors, or to the actual lives of the fools and idiots themselves. And such writings as do exist describe not so much the social realities of the existence of idiots as changes in scientific and religious ideas. With the coming of the nineteenth and twentieth centuries, however, it is possible to present a much more detailed picture of the relationship between ideas about idiocy and developments of a social and practical nature.

THE NINETEENTH-CENTURY REFORMS

In the early nineteenth century, provision for the education and care of idiots was made for the first time on more than a purely individual basis. Before the end of the eighteenth century, their education was not a matter of public concern or debate. The question of whether and how idiots could be improved first attracted notice through the experiments of the Frenchman, Itard, with a 'savage' boy whom he called Victor. This issue has remained a central one ever since, with Itard's work a central reference point for many subsequent writers.

Early educationalists assumed that all idiots were capable of some improvement, even if they could not be cured. As Seguin declared in 1846: 'While waiting for medicine to cure idiots, I have undertaken to see that they participate in the benefit of education.'[19] And an anonymous article written in the *Edinburgh Review* in 1865 claims: 'All cannot be equally improved, but it is rare to discover a single instance where some benefit is not imparted.'[20]

The energies of the people who set up the first schools and asylums for idiots were directed more towards finding successful methods of education and towards convincing the public to provide funds, than to the investigation of causes. Such concern was not to come until later. Many claims for the humanity of idiots were made specifically within the context of proposals for their education and thus the promise of their improvement. 'The immortal soul is essentially the same in every creature born of woman' – thus said Guggenbühl, the founder of the first European residential school for idiots.[21] 'Human beings with veiled powers' is another description in one of the first English books on teaching methods.[22]

Seguin made quite categorical statements on the essential humanity of idiots: 'An idiot is endowed with moral nature and is influenced by the same things as the rest of humanity'; 'one of us in mankind but shut up in an imperfect envelope'; 'an innocent isolated without associations'.[23] This view was reiterated in the *Edinburgh Review* article. Welcoming the 'uniformly successful experiment of ameliorating the state of the idiot', the author asserts: 'There is mind in all these wretched people, its manifestations only hindered by a defective organism' – as though it might easily be thought there wasn't.[24]

Although such claims about the humanity of idiots were part of the reforming initiative of the mid-nineteenth century, they were made in such a way as to keep alive the possibility that idiots might not in fact be fully human. Frequent comparisons between

idiots and animals were made by those who were also the main
advocates of their education and who were the most intent on
claiming them for humanity. Despite his convictions concerning
their moral nature, Seguin describes them as

... fashioned in the shape of man, but shorn of all other human attri-
butes, breathing masses of flesh ... These unfortunates not only are
endowed with the animal instincts and propensities, but with the feeble
germs of those better qualities which are super-added to our physical
nature, and which could never occur in the best-trained lower animal,
even if its perceptive faculties were more acute than theirs.

In this wreck of powers, one human irresistible tendency or impulse
is left him; for as low as we find him, lower than the brute in regard to
activity and intelligence, he has, as the great, the lowly, the privileged,
the millions, his hobby or amulet that no animal has: the external thing
towards which his human centrifugal power gravitates. This shows he
can form of himself a connection with the outside world or can be
helped to do so.[25]

Thus, for Seguin the purpose of their education is to lift them
from such a near-animal state: 'There is not one of any age who
may not be made more of a man and less of a brute by patience
and kindness directed by energy and skill.'[26] A similar aim, 'The
removal of the mark of the brute from the forehead of the idiot'
is quoted in 1895 by Shuttleworth, superintendent of the Royal
Albert Asylum in Lancaster.[27] Reference to the 'animal nature'
of idiots is also made in 1848 by Howe, America's leading advocate of their public education. 'The lower the degree of endow-
ment, the more nearly the look approaches that of animals.'[28]

This ambivalence about the place of idiots in mankind, an
opposition between their actual, somewhat animal state and their
potential humanity, is the basis on which the case for their
education was made to depend. The justification for reform in the
treatment of idiots in terms of their possible transformation into
more socially acceptable people has been one of the main arguments of reformers ever since.

Before the beginning of the nineteenth century, the arguments
had turned on whether idiots were similar to other people in
God's eyes, whether they had a spiritual nature and soul that
would survive death. The acceptance of idiots as part of mankind

irrespective of what they could be made into is also to be found in some later philanthropic writings. For example, Bateman refers, in 1897, to 'the imperishable essence' within them, and their spiritual capacity as evidence of their inclusion in the 'human family'.[29] But generally speaking the humanity of idiots was tied to their possible improvement through education. It is a double-edged connection which continues to the present.

The enthusiasm and hope surrounding the early asylums and schools appear remarkable, now that we can see how they later developed. Buildings that now fill us with despair were seen as model environments, full of promise. A sense of what might be achieved is found in the following description of the opening of a small asylum in 1850:

The first gathering of the idiotic family was a spectacle unique in itself, sufficiently discouraging to the most resolved, and not to be forgotten in after time by any. It was a period of distraction, disorder, and noise of the most unnatural character. Some had defective sight; most had defective or no utterance; most were lame in limb or muscle; and all were of weak and perverted mind. Some had been spoiled, some neglected, and some ill-used. Some were clamorous and rebellious; some were sullen and perverse; and some unconscious and inert. Some were screaming at the top of the voice; some making constant and involuntary noises from nervous irritation; and some, terrified at scorn and ill-treatment, hid themselves in a corner from the face of man, as the face of an enemy. Windows were smashed, wainscoting broken, boundaries defied and the spirit of mischief and disobedience prevailed. Some who witnessed the scene retired from it in disgust and others in despair. How very different the impression is at present many can testify. Here is now order, obedience to authority, classification, improvement and cheerful occupation. Every hour has its duties; and these duties are steadily fulfilled. Windows are now safe, boundaries are observed without rules, and doors are safe without locks. The desire now is not to get away but to stay. They are essentially now not only an improving family but a *happy family*. And all this is secured without the aid of *correction* or *coercion* . . .[30]

Other contemporary accounts emphasize the cheerful and kind nature of the new asylums:

Nothing more surprises a visitor to a well-managed asylum for imbeciles than the entire absence of that gloom which most persons naturally expect to find hanging over it like a dark cloud ... everything is done that can make learning enjoyable, and the powers are never overtaxed by dwelling on one thing too long ... All the fittings of the room have a tendency to keep the pupils in a state of pleasant feeling ... Even the feeblest seem calm and contented.[31]

Force of any kind was considered repugnant; patience and firmness on the part of teachers was frequently recommended. 'The only key to the intelligence of the unfortunate children is that of affection which leads to respect and obedience ...'[32] Psychiatry generally at the time was concerned with 'moral' treatment and therefore with a rejection of physical coercion and brutality. In moral treatment the will of a patient has to be harnessed and induced to regulate his or her behaviour more harmoniously. For Seguin, a teacher's authority over a child was derived from similar principles: 'The aim of education is liberty and the first condition of being free is willpower and obedience and authority are its preconditions ... The will of the teacher is important in commanding the weaker will of the child – he will not, but we will for him.'[33]

Many useful and leisure occupations were provided, as well as formal instruction. The importance of good health, hygiene, nutrition and exercise was frequently emphasized. Bodily improvement was seen as the key to mental improvement – an idea which occurs in almost every text on the subject:

The body is but the instrument, the mind, the unseen musician, and the strings must be in tune or no harmony can be produced by the most skilful hand. Thus the corporal state of the idiot being disordered, discord results from the agency of the mind upon it ... As the body condition is abnormal, so is the manifestation of mind in idiots.[34]

Sensory and muscular development formed the basis of Seguin's new educational methods, which reflected contemporary assumptions about the relationships between mind and body: 'Idiots require more room, air, warmth and light to improve their weak and sluggish natures.'[35]

The value of the asylum in bringing idiots together out of their former solitude is often mentioned along with the observation that the original Greek word for idiot meant literally a solitary person. Some accounts mentioned how idiot children had been kept locked away by their parents, and an American report makes the following observations:

> ... an imbecile child at home has a tendency to solitude or exclusiveness; it cannot play with other children ... it is a lonely being ... It needs to be with those who are like itself ... this association provided friction and friction produces growth. There is an unconscious self-culture resulting from the mere force of association. In this lies one secret of the success in institutions for the feeble-minded.[36]

Many new educational methods were developed, mostly inspired by Seguin, but also growing from the experience of the teachers themselves. The detailed accounts are remarkable for their similarity in content to much of what is written now. Psychologists in the last twenty years have had to rediscover much of what was already known and practised by the 1860s; it is difficult not to feel that if many of these early educational recommendations were put into practice now, we would achieve more than we have done so far. The insight was commonplace that whereas most ordinary children can learn if they are left alone, 'imperfect' children cannot and therefore need structured learning situations. The roles of imitation, repetition and reward in learning are all described, as was the importance of developing the imagination through play.[37] Descriptions of speech training procedures sound very similar to those now advocated by behaviour modification theorists. Many educationalists, particularly Seguin, were very conscious that their new methods would benefit the teaching of ordinary children, citing especially the frequent changes of activity, the emphasis on sensory and bodily functions, the analysis of tasks into their components and the absence of physical coercion.

Writings of the mid and late nineteenth century are also full of case histories – stories of success, individually illustrated. There was a general recognition that some idiots might be too hopeless to be much improved, that the best that could be done was to ensure their physical improvement and comfort: these contemporary reports mostly paint a picture of considerable achievement, made concrete through the specific examples, even if difficult to assess in terms of overall numbers. One account describes the achievements of Earlswood Asylum, 'Thus the solitary and useless are made social and industrious, while relieved of the blight of their deplorable condition they become conscious of their humanity, as well as in a measure independent, happy and confident, instead of helpless, sad and distrustful.'[38]

That the promise of these early institutions was not fulfilled is highly significant, and it is important for us to understand why not. For these asylums subsequently developed into the repressive and custodial institutions whose legacy is with us now, despite the benevolent intentions of the early reformers, and despite their assertions of the potential if not actual humanity of idiots. Idiots themselves came to be regarded as less than fully human, a scourge and a danger to human society.

THE FAILURE OF REFORM

Virtually all nineteenth-century writers comment on the growing number of idiots. The numbers in idiot asylums grew from approximately 400 in 1864 to about 2,000 in 1914; but during most of this period there were only six such asylums and these contained only a small proportion of the total numbers.[39] The majority of idiots, estimated at 29,452 in 1881 for England and Wales, were to be found in other public institutions – workhouses and asylums for the insane.[40]

The contemporary authors tended to see the increase in numbers of idiots as a real increase in the numbers born, a reflection, as they thought, of the ravages of modern civilization. However, the apparent increase may well have consisted in an increase in the numbers of idiots coming to the attention of the various authorities, no longer contained within their families. Certainly, the increase in numbers requiring institutional care was not confined to idiocy – the much larger and earlier growth of asylums for the insane was accompanied by dramatic rises in the apparent numbers of lunatics. There are many reasons why the number of idiots coming to the attention of the authorities may have increased, as will be discussed below, but one contributing factor may have been the very creation of asylums: the provision of services can itself stimulate demand. Furthermore, there was increasingly a widening of the definition of idiocy, to incorporate those regarded as feeble-minded – the people who were to fill the asylums of the early twentieth century.

The asylums themselves grew in size. Seguin and all the initial reformers anticipated a much higher rate of return of inmates to their communities than in fact took place. The original asylums were never conceived of as life-long institutions, rather as places where idiots could be trained for a period of years, for as long as they made visible progress. However, there was often nowhere for idiots to return to: families were scattered and untraceable, or unable to accept back an idiot member, however well trained. And sometimes the expected improvements did not materialize. Under such conditions of increasing admissions and life-long residence, the asylums changed. Certainly Seguin considered small size essential to his educational goals: in 1870 he explicitly warned against the evils of over-growth that he saw in other institutions.

However, the increasing size of asylums is not a complete explanation for the deterioration in standards that took place. It should have been possible to maintain a higher standard of care and education had the desire to do so been present, and had the resources been made available, which increasingly they were not.

The seeds of future repression are to be found partly in the ideas and activities of the reformers themselves. Many initial ideas about asylums, whilst put forward in a spirit of reform, were in fact open to all kinds of abuse. The principles of moral treatment, progressive as they were in contrast to the brutal physical treatment of the eighteenth century, could be used all too easily against rather than for the interests of its subjects.[41] From Seguin's 'He will not, but we will for him', it is but a short step to the total domination of the child by the teacher. The emphasis on will-power and obedience was to turn into conformity to a rigid discipline.

The carefully designed environments and daily programmes enabled the smallest detail of each inmate's life to be brought under the control and inspection of the attendants and teachers. From this it was not far to an excessive regimentation of inmates and a complete lack of personal privacy. Collecting idiots together as a means of alleviating their solitude and isolation was to evolve into the mass organization of their daily life and the denial of their individuality, conditions that are still with us. Moral treatment came to provide an efficient means of managing large numbers of inmates.

Increasingly, medical men became the managers of the new asylums, despite the fact that it had been lay reformers and educationalists who had taken the initiative in setting them up. In the case of the insane asylums, a similar transition to complete medical control only took place in the face of much opposition from the lay reformers.[42] In the case of the idiot asylums, there are few records of any public debate about the suitability of medical control, but by the last quarter of the century doctors were firmly in charge. Their interest is reflected in the spate of new books published containing descriptions, classifications and attempted diagnoses of the numerous idiots assembled together for the first time in the asylums.

The development of asylums must also be seen in the context of the rapid social changes that took place in the lives of ordinary people in the eighteenth and nineteenth centuries. It is commonly assumed that it was pure humanitarian concern for the education and welfare of idiots that motivated the setting up of the first schools and asylums. But to suppose that it was either this or the 'spirit' of the French Revolution that led to such a benevolent interest in idiots, would be to look only at the ideas involved, and not at the social forces that generated such ideas.[43] Rather, the attention of reformers was drawn to the problem of idiocy, as well as to many others, as a result of the heavy strains – in some cases amounting virtually to social collapse – brought to bear on family life by the wide-ranging industrial reorganization of work.

Public institutions of all kinds – for the old, sick, insane, criminal, young – were built in increasing numbers and sizes throughout the nineteenth century; the growth of idiot asylums was part of this enormous social change. The question of the social origins of asylums in general is vast and beyond the scope of this book, but some indication can be given of the framework needed to fully understand the rise of idiot asylums.

The nineteenth-century rise of asylums signifies a change from local and family based attempts to contain and support disruptive or dependent people, to larger scale public provision. This involved the removal of such people from on-going life, and their collection together in specially designed environments, where they could be reformed or cured. In the case of America, Rothman, in *The Discovery of the Asylum*, suggests this change from local to institutional solutions was part of a panic reaction to the rapidly changing world of the late eighteenth and early nineteenth century.[44] The new institutions, with their carefully planned architecture and detailed regimes of life, seemed to promise a controlled and model environment that would not only reform their inmates but would also provide a prototype for a new social order.

In England also, the rise of specialist asylums signified an important shift in the way in which the poor, dependent and deviant were contained, as A. Scull describes in *Museums of Madness*.[45] Public workhouses, as opposed to domestic relief, were increasingly used for all those who could not or would not support themselves economically. In these, idiots, lunatics, the chronic sick, the old and vagrants were mixed up with the allegedly able-bodied unemployed. But in order to effectively discipline (and deter) the latter, those whom it was thought could be forced to work, it became necessary to segregate those who could not help being dependent and whose behaviour often disrupted the discipline of the workhouse. Many different kinds of deviance became differentiated on a wide scale, and specialist asylums and professions grew accordingly.

Asylums of all kinds were seen as positive reforming forces, instruments of social change – not, as they are now, places of last resort. In the case of idiot asylums, the healthy sociable world of the institution was frequently contrasted to the isolated and wretched conditions of working-class family life, its order and discipline to the lack of order and education in most communities.[46] As we have seen, the early educationalists also made a point of emphasizing that their methods could be used as a model to improve the education of all children, not just the idiots.

The changes in work and family life brought about by the

Industrial Revolution radically affected the position of anyone who was dependent on others for economic and social support. The shift in work to factory-based production had many implications for the position of women and children. The chaos and near-disintegration of working-class family life, as a result of the concentration of people in large cities, and of the demands of work, has often been described. For idiots this must have meant severe suffering, since they could no longer be either integrated into work of any kind or supported within the family. While it may once have been in a family's interest to teach an idiot child some useful work and social skills, it was hardly the same for a factory owner, with his eye on quick production and profit, and with an easily replaceable work-force. The speed of factory work, the enforced discipline, the time-keeping and production norms – all these were a highly unfavourable change from the slower, more self-determined and flexible methods of work into which many handicapped people had been integrated.

So an idiot child could no longer be so easily looked after, supervised or taught at home. Since all members of the family who could went out to work, an adult or older child staying at home just to look after an idiot would mean an intolerable loss of earnings for the family, as is often commented on in contemporary textbooks. Idiots were, therefore, often left alone, locked up, or turned out on to the streets.

The asylums of the nineteenth century were thus as much the result of far-reaching changes in work and family life, and corresponding methods of containing the poor, as they were the inspiration of philanthropists and scientists. With other similar institutions of the period, they have remained as the main alternative to the family ever since.

The hopes of the reformers were often expressed, as we have seen, in terms of education – how it could change the individual idiot into a worthwhile, happy and useful person. The danger of such an approach is that if for any reason the expected improvement does not take place, then the way is left open for concluding that idiots are not so human after all.

This is why the 'failure' of the first schools and asylums in not returning all their inmates to some kind of normal life outside has

so often been attributed to the hopeless nature of the idiots themselves, as well as to the allegedly unrealistic ideas that their
educators had about improvements. In fact the mistake that was
made – and continues to be made – was to suppose that a transformation could be brought about by education alone. The early
educationalists' real failure was in not sufficiently appreciating the
nature of a society that created the growing need for asylums
and that made it extremely difficult for so many people, let alone
idiots, to survive. Their mistake was not so much in the content
of their ideas about education, as in their belief in the power of
these ideas, divorced in their implementation from either social
reality or social action.

The inevitable conclusion in the nineteenth century was that it
was the idiot that was at fault, that he was not worth such expenditure of resources, and that he was unable to live anything
but a segregated and custodial life.

THE DEHUMANIZATION OF IDIOTS

In the ideas that subsequently developed about idiots and the
practices that these ideas led to, it is possible to observe the
emergence of increasing dehumanization. No longer seen as a
personal misfortune, idiocy came to be regarded as a widespread
social evil.

One of the earliest writers to see idiocy as a social threat was
Howe, usually regarded as one of America's leading humanitarian
reformers. In 1848 he wrote *On the Causes of Idiocy* as part of his
campaign to persuade the Massachusetts legislature to provide
funds for a residential training school for idiots, and his ideas
were subsequently very influential in England.

Seeing idiocy as 'part of the host of social evils which society is
in vain trying to hold off by jails, almhouses etc.', Howe laid the
blame squarely at the feet of parents; their drunkenness, masturbation, inter-marriage, attempts at abortion, fright and ill
health were all violations of 'natural laws'. Such violations, in
combination rather than singly, could result in an idiot child.

It was Howe who introduced the concept of a general predisposition or hereditary tendency to idiocy in certain families which subsequently dominated the history of ideas about idiocy. As evidence, he claimed 359 cases of idiocy, in all but 4 of which he could find deviations from healthy living on the part of the parents:

The moral to be drawn from the existence of the individual idiot is this – he, or his parents, have so far violated the natural laws, so far marred the beautiful organism of the body, that it is an unfit manifestation of the powers of the soul. The moral to be drawn from the prevalent existence of idiocy in society is that a very large class of persons ignore the conditions upon which alone health and reason are given to men, and consequently they sin in various ways.[47]

Howe's speculation on the origins of idiocy thus situates supposedly biological facts – organic damage to the bodies of parents, leading to reduced bodily and mental vigour in the child – within a religious and moral framework. Such evil is punishment for sins that have to be atoned for. This admixture of the moral and the biological was to persist throughout the nineteenth and twentieth century.

Seguin saw idiots somewhat differently, although still in a religious and social framework. At the opening of a school for idiots in Syracuse in 1854, he criticized those who considered idiots to be an evil and a punishment from God, preferring to see their potential benefit to mankind: 'God has scattered among us, rare as the possessors of talent or genius, the idiot, the blind, the deaf-mute, in order to bind the talented to the incapable, the rich to the needy, all men to each other, by a tie of indissoluble solidarity.'[48]

Later, however, with the growing realization that idiot schools and asylums were not escaping the adverse consequences of increasing numbers, even Seguin turned to blame, though never to the extent of other nineteenth-century writers. Remarking, as they all do, on the apparent increase in idiocy, he asks what new causes there might be and identifies the changing status of women as a likely source: 'As soon as women assumed the anxieties pertaining to both sexes they gave birth to children whose like had hardly been met with thirty years ago.'[49] The changing aspirations of women 'has not taught them anything of womanhood'; other women 'are over-anxious about being a good wife' and altogether 'the foetus has no place to grow in peace'.

Seguin's radicalism clearly did not extend to the situation of women, nor to the aspirations of nineteenth-century feminists. Despite his general concern for the oppressed, even Seguin did not have a sufficiently deep understanding of the social changes that were affecting the position of all dependent people and their families and apparently causing an increase in the number of idiots. This failure led him, like others, to scapegoat one particular group of people as being to blame.

From the 1860s onwards, the collecting together of idiots in asylums made more possible the systematic study of different types and causes of idiocy. Interest grew in developmental causes and hereditary influences, and new conceptualizations of the differences between idiots (or mental defectives as they became known) and the rest of mankind were proposed.

Writers of the new medical textbooks tended to follow Howe's view that idiots represented the evils of society in the form of their parents' transgressions. Ireland, superintendent of a Scottish asylum, wrote in 1877: 'There can be no doubt of the great part played by heredity in the genesis of idiocy. Idiots frequently are born in families in which there is a decided neurotic tendency, as manifested by the appearance of insanity, imbecility, or epilepsy among the members.'[50] Seeing idiocy as particularly prevalent in a society 'struggling under unhealthy and disquieting influences' he follows Seguin in singling out the changing status of women and their nervous exhaustion as leading to children 'conceived in antagonism'. On the other hand he disagrees with Howe's indictment of alcoholism as a major factor.

Shuttleworth, superintendent of the Royal Albert Asylum, in a survey of more than 2,000 cases concluded that idiocy is caused not by a single factor but by many contributory ones, what he calls 'repeated transgressions' of the parents: 'Not every drunken parent procreates an idiot, but when inherited nervous instability from this or other causes is intensified in the next generation by injudicious marriage or by unfavourable environment, instances of mental degeneracy are apt to occur.'[51]

Bateman, physician at the Eastern Counties Asylum, views

idiocy as '... an expression of parental defects and vices ... a result of the violation of natural laws over several generations ... people ignore conditions of health and reason, pervert their natural appetites ...'[52] He claims that a large proportion of idiots have alcoholic parents or insane relatives. And once again women who step outside their customary role are blamed: '... a female mathematical athlete is unsuited for the duties and responsibilities of maternity ... the mental endowments of her children are likely to be below the average.'

Tredgold takes the emphasis on heredity even further, claiming in 1908 that 90 per cent of all mental defectives were the result of 'inherent defects in germinal plasm.'[53] And a later textbook describes most forms of mental deficiency as being due to 'intrinsic causes' or 'morbid heredity.'[54]

Some medical textbooks included descriptions of idiots in which they were likened to allegedly more primitive non-European people. The most famous and most persistent racist classification is that of Langdon-Down, who identified one distinct sub-group of idiots as Mongolian: it was 'difficult to realize he [the idiot] is the child of Europeans'; there was 'no doubt that these ethnic features are the result of degeneration'.[55]

Other classifications were even more fanciful. Tredgold, for example, thought he could distinguish Negroid, Grecian, Egyptian and American-Indian types of mental defective. This ethnic form of classification was not some quirk of the writers concerned, but was put forward at a time of great interest in the biological evolution of mankind and of the increasing British colonization of hitherto 'uncivilized' parts of the world. Idiots were seen as unfinished and primitive forms of man, like savages in their nearness to nature and their distance from the heights of European civilization. Anthropology of the period is full of attempts to place the various tribes and races in evolutionary order, according to how primitive and ape-like they appeared. This classification system was applied also to the medical study of mental deficiency.

Idiots were seen as manifestations of the 'lower nature' of civilized man, barely kept under control by the forces of society. As one asylum superintendent observed in 1895: 'When the inhibitive nerve power is weakened, the lower nature is apt to assert itself. Though children in mind they are very often men and women in wickedness and vice.'[56] And an American doctor, Barr, wrote in 1904: 'The sexual desires [in mental defectives] are exaggerated in proportion to the animal over the psychic forces ... the organs of reproduction are fully developed, in men they are even enlarged.'[57]

The so-called animal nature of idiots had previously been conceived of as incompetence and lack of rationality. Now their animality was pictured more as uncivilized, as the allegedly uncontrollable forces of instinct and desire that late Victorian society was in general very concerned to repress. This shift reflects the contemporary Victorian identification of sexuality with the more animal part of human nature, as well as what was considered to be a conflict between civilization and nature – the former being achieved only at the cost of the latter. Even those such as Bateman, who argued strongly against the idea that idiots were half-way between apes and man, saw idiots as particularly prone to sin.

The enormous sense of difference between idiots and the rest of society is expressed in Tredgold's definition: 'Amentia is not a subtraction in varying degrees from normal ... the two conditions do not merge into each other ... instead there is a great and impassable gulf ... they have no intelligence, and no consciousness of pleasure and pain; in fact their mental state is one entire negation.'[58]

Now the animal nature of idiots, once an insult to humanity and something to be pitied, became a danger. Idiots were thought to revel in their brutishness. Added to the racist typologies, this idea led easily to the notion that idiots were a degeneration of the purity of the human (i.e. European) race. And from there it was but a short step to demands for their control – particularly control over their reproduction. Notions of physical degeneracy merged with those of immorality and crime. Idiots came to be regarded as both the result, and increasingly the bearers, of all kinds of social degeneration: alcoholism, masturbation, poverty, thieving, illegitimacy etc. By the early twentieth century it was to be society itself rather than the individual idiot which needed freeing from the degradations of idiocy.

An indiscriminate linking of mental deficiency with all kinds of social problems became commonplace. In 1896 the National Association for the Care and Control of the Feeble Minded was set up and began to function as a pressure group for the lifetime segregation of defectives. Their emphasis on the prevention of sexuality and reproduction was motivated by middle-class fears about working-class fertility, greatly fuelled by the Eugenics Movement's scaremongering about the likely decline in the talents of the British people.

In 1908 the Radnor Commission, set up to make legislative recommendations, reported:

Of the gravity of the present state of things, there is no doubt. The mass of facts collected, the statements of our witnesses, and our own personal visits and investigations compel the conclusion that there are numbers of mentally defective persons whose training is neglected, over whom no sufficient control is exercised, and whose wayward and irresponsible lives are productive of crime and misery, of much injury and mischief to themselves, and of much continuous expenditure wasteful to the community and to individual families ... The Royal Commission devoted much attention to the causation of mental defect, and arrived at the conclusion that feeble-mindedness is largely inherited; that prevention of mentally defective persons from becoming parents would tend to diminish the number of such persons in the population; and that consequently there are strong grounds for placing mental defectives of each sex in institutions where they will be retained and kept under effectual supervision as long as may be necessary ... As respects [however] congenital and incurable forms of mental defect ... the remedy is to place persons so suffering under such restrictions as to make procreation impossible.[59]

During the 1910 general election, the National Association for the Care and Control of the Feeble Minded campaigned vigorously on this issue of 'discouraging parenthood in feeble-minded and other degenerate types' and for the building of separate institutions.[60] In 1913 the Mental Deficiency Act introduced compulsory certification for people admitted to institutions as mentally defective. This Act established the basis of a separate and unified service, which would exclude mental defective people from other welfare and social agencies as well as from the general education system.

Control and care were to be established by a system of either guardianship and supervision in the community or in institutions called 'colonies', with a central Board of Control. In the case of higher-grade adults, social deviance, i.e. committing any kind of crime or having an illegitimate child, became grounds for compulsory supervision, certification or confinement in an institution.

The Act was slow to be implemented, and in 1929 the report of the Wood Committee underlined the fact that mental defectives were still seen as a continued threat:

Let us assume that we could segregate as a separate community all the families in this country containing mental defectives of the primary amentia type. We should find that we had collected among them a most interesting social group. It would include, as everyone who has extensive practical experience of social service would readily admit, a much larger proportion of insane persons, epileptics, paupers, criminals (especially recedivists), unemployables, habitual slum dwellers, prostitutes, inebriates and other social inefficients than would a group of families not containing mental defectives. The overwhelming majority of the families thus collected will belong to the section of the community which we propose to term the 'social problem' or 'subnormal group'. This group comprises approximately the lowest 10 per cent in the social scale of most communities . . . If we are to prevent the racial disaster of mental deficiency we must deal not merely with the mentally defective persons, but with the whole subnormal group from which the majority of them come. Primary amentia may be, and often is, an end result – the last stage of the inheritance of degeneracy of this subnormal group. The relative fertility of this (subnormal) group is greater than that of normal persons . . .[61]

These eugenic fears persisted despite the findings of a contemporary survey that only 7.6 per cent of the patients of one particular asylum had defective parents themselves.[62] The Board of Control was undeterred and stated in 1930:

On racial grounds the undesirability of allowing defectives to marry is too obvious to need elaboration. It is true that too little is known of the extent to which mental defect is transmissible to allow of any precise calculations of the proportion of the offspring of such marriage who will themselves be defectives or who will be 'carriers' of a hereditary taint. But no one who has any practical experience needs to be warned of the racial danger of breeding from tainted stock ... On these grounds our Board have in previous Reports strongly recommended that the marriage of defectives under Order should be prohibited by law ...[63]

And the psychologist, Burt, added his characteristically scaremongering note: 'Defectives of both sexes, it is urged, are liable to propagate deficiency, and that at a geometrically increasing rate.'[64]

Another report of 1934 once again blamed women, unmarried defective women in particular, for producing a high proportion of all defective children.[65] This report, like that of the Board of Control, recommended legislation to ensure the 'voluntary' sterilization of mentally defective women. Although such legislation has never actually been passed in England, unlike America where sterilization became compulsory in many states, this has not prevented many such operations from being carried out in this country under various forms of coercion.

Ideas of degeneration have persisted, notably in the Nazi extermination of hundreds of thousands of mentally handicapped people, in the name of the purity of the Aryan race. The National Front uses similar propaganda against mentally handicapped people. The spectre of animality is still raised: a popular book by a well-known psychiatrist refers to the crude and primitive habits of idiots and claims that they '... are in fact considerably less intelligent than domestic animals.'[66] Imbeciles supposedly have 'disastrous' responses to sexual or aggressive 'impulses' and may commit murder, rape or arson.

After World War I a large number of new asylums were built, and between 1918 and 1931 the number of places in institutions registered under the Mental Deficiency Act nearly tripled. In the eight years that followed it nearly doubled again, to reach 32,000 by 1939.[67] On the other hand services outside the asylums developed more slowly. In spite of an increase in guardianship and supervision orders, the number of day and occupation centres for those excluded from ordinary or special schools remained very small. Nor was very much invested in community services of any other kind.

IQ FATALISM

A further direction in which ideas about idiocy changed was an increasing emphasis on the hopeless and incurable nature of the condition. Because the previously accepted distinction between 'incurable' and 'unimprovable' became blurred, interest and enthusiasm in education waned, although many writers continued to endorse the importance of training in acceptable moral and religious behaviour and useful habits.

This shift reflected new psychological notions about mental competence arising from the imposition in the 1870s of universal education and subsequent invention in 1908 of IQ tests. The assumptions of these tests, namely that the IQ was a measure of a fixed potential with which each individual was born and which determined his or her educability, meant that mental defectives were classed as having very little potential and thus as being hardly educable.

Binet and Simon, French psychologists and the originators of IQ tests, were more than merely critical of Seguin and his hopeful idealism: they also asserted confidently that many mental defectives were ineducable, needing therefore medical supervision rather than education.[68] The apotheosis of the IQ approach would ultimately be found in Burt's definition in 1935 of mental deficiency as '... an innate deficiency in innate intellectual capacity, or briefly, a defect of intelligence'.[69]

Burt's definition is in many ways nonsensical but this has not prevented his views from having an enormous influence on educational thinking and practice.[70] According to such definitions, mental defectives could not be made more intelligent and so belief in their capacity to learn anything tended to be very small and thus the importance of education in their lives – particularly of the more severely defective – was minimized.

Their permanently hopeless state was held to warrant their complete segregation and this was given legislative expression in the 1913 Act. In the words of a contemporary report: 'This Act is a public recognition that congenital mental defect is practically incurable, that it is essential that persons so suffering should both in their own interests and that of the community be placed under proper supervision . . .'[71]

The treatment of the mentally deficient has been dominated by the IQ definition throughout the twentieth century – a domination that is conceptual, diagnostic and administrative. In theory, the difference between mental defectives and others is conceived of as one of degree rather than kind, since the IQ test assumes a continuum of intelligence from subnormal through normal to supernormal. It might be supposed that the exclusion of the subnormal from the rest of society would be lessened by this conception, as opposed to one which maintained a radical difference in kind between subnormal and normal. In practice, however, this notion of a continuum of intelligence has been quite compatible with – and in fact used to maintain – an extreme degree of segregation from society, an almost total rejection. In providing an allegedly objective means of diagnosis, the IQ test has been used as a formal dividing line between normal and subnormal.

The introduction of the IQ also allowed many more distinctions to be made between mental defectives themselves, according to grade. Such distinctions were not new to the twentieth century. As early as the seventeenth century Willis had observed 'stupidity hath many degrees – for some are accounted unfit and incapable as to all things, and others to some things only . . .', going on to detail the different levels of skill and ability he himself had observed in fools.[72] In the nineteenth century similar distinctions used both behavioural criteria – what activities the various levels of idiot were capable of – and more theoretical notions – the degree to which the nervous system was seen to be in control of the body, for example.[73] Distinctions were also acknowledged in how amenable various idiots were to improvement.

The developments of the twentieth century took this categorization a major step further in the division which was made between educable and ineducable defectives. IQ measurements were the basis of this division, those with an IQ of less than 50 being regarded as ineducable and necessitating formal exclusion from education (under the provisions of various Mental Deficiency Acts). The 'educable' defectives were, as children, mainly provided for through the education system, in the special schools or classes created during the first quarter of the century. The 'ineducable' ones were regarded as a medical responsibility, at best trainable. They were consigned to the asylums and colonies, and, after World War II, to the occupation and training centres run by local health authorities. Medicine, either in the form of the hospitals or the local health departments, was made the repository of the most hopeless, those discarded even by the special education system, as well as of the most troublesome, those regarded as unfit for society.

Within psychology the IQ definition led to a completely one-dimensional view of mentally deficient people. They were seen only in terms of their IQs (or the equivalent, their mental ages). Countless experiments, and a whole theoretical approach, were based on the hypothesis that it is meaningful to identify and group together people on the basis of common low IQ scores and then to compare them with higher IQ groups. Differences between people with the same IQ scores were ignored. The basis of the comparisons was not questioned, not even the extremely narrow range of qualities that the IQ test measured.[74]

SOCIAL AND BIOLOGICAL CATEGORIES

A second important development in the biological sciences was also to have its effect on ideas about the causes of mental subnormality. In the nineteenth and early twentieth century the phrase 'hereditary tendency' was used to describe almost any trait that could be related to the supposed defects of parents or other relatives and that was present from childhood. But the discoveries of Mendelian genetics and the increasing knowledge of embryonic development made such an over-inclusive notion less and less tenable. At least this was the case among people who claimed to be scientific and objective; as late as 1935 Burt was still attempting to combine together the vast range of genetic, congenital, developmental and familial disorders in one category of 'innate' deficiency, which he then described as 'inherited'.

The Wood Committee report of 1929 did, however, reflect to some extent the changing views on the causation of mental deficiency. It introduced a distinction between two kinds of defective, those whose defects could be regarded as purely biological and those who were considered to be part of a sub-cultural social group without any clear organic pathology. This distinction was based on an IQ conception of intelligence. The sub-cultural group represented the bottom end of the 'normal' distribution of IQ scores, due to the ordinary variation that would be expected among any group of people. The biological or pathological group was seen as a consequence of various exceptional biological accidents, superimposed on the normal curve of IQ scores.

The pathological group supposedly formed the excess number of mental defectives with very low IQ scores, i.e. the excess over the numbers predicted by the normal distribution of IQ scores. This excess was simply assumed, never really verified; indeed many studies have reported dramatically fewer mentally handicapped people than predicted by IQ statistics.[75] The pathological group had a social-class composition that was representative of the whole population in contrast to the sub-cultural group which came exclusively from working-class backgrounds and which tended to have many relatives with low IQ scores as well.

The effect of this distinction was to separate those mental defectives of clear medical interest from those about whom medicine had little to say diagnostically, but who were regarded as a social problem. As such the distinction does at least reflect the real growth of more precise scientific knowledge: former generalized views about 'hereditary tendencies' could no longer be applied to the whole range of mental defectives, especially not to those 'biological accidents', with specific pathological syndromes and intelligent parents. It also signifies the removal of a section of the mentally defective population from indiscriminate association with other social problems, a suspension of blame from some (often middle-class) parents. Yet although the generalized blaming of parents had to be modified in the face of increasing scientific knowledge, it did reappear in the indictment of families of higher grade working-class defectives. These were the ones whose 'diagnosis' had been particularly facilitated by the invention of IQ tests and whose 'discovery' gave rise to such panic and repression. Their low intelligence was ascribed to their poor 'inheritance' from their parents.

Attempts to distinguish between two groups of mentally handicapped people, based on either class differences or the presence or absence of organic pathology, are still with us. In its American form the distinction 'organic' versus 'cultural-familial' (instead of pathological versus sub-cultural) is frequently found in textbooks on mental handicap, postulated as though soundly based. The 'cultural-familial' are even called 'garden variety' defectives.

Jensen particularly makes use of the distinction, both to back up his arguments for the high heritability of IQ, and to attempt to prove a genetically based difference between the learning processes of retarded children with different IQ scores and different racial and class backgrounds. 'Cultural-familial retardation', he claims, 'is predominantly concentrated in the lower social classes.'[76]

Not only the evidence on which this distinction is based, but also the attribution of high heritability to 'cultural-familial' retardation are both extremely dubious. To begin with, the supposed absence of any organic pathology is very much a question of the present state of scientific knowledge and investigations made in any particular case. Moreover, the data that purport to prove differences in family incidence of low IQ scores according to the grade of mental deficiency have been hotly disputed. The main study on which Jensen relies to prove these differences has fundamental flaws in the ways in which information was selected and computed.[77] Finally, there has been a large amount of empirical research which fails to find any actual differences between these two groups and thus throws serious doubt on the reality of the distinction at all.[78] Whilst claiming always to be more scientific and objective than his opponents, Jensen, in fact, is using some of the most socially biased and unsound categorizations that science has thrown up.

One of the significant effects of scientific interest in mentally handicapped people is a tendency to evaluate them in terms of clinical and behavioural symptoms and a consequent relative neglect of either their subjective experience or social existence. Since World War II, the identification of mentally deficient people as a widespread social threat has given way to an ideology that characterizes them as sick and useless. This redefinition is reflected in the legislation passed in the Mental Health Act of 1959, which distinguished 'subnormality' from 'psychopathy', thereby dividing off those who were regarded as social threats (whatever their intelligence level) from those who simply suffered from low intelligence. Definitions became increasingly medical, as the Act reflects: 'Subnormality means a state of arrested and incomplete development of mind . . . of a nature and degree which is susceptible to medical treatment or other special care or training of the patient.'[79] In this definition the mentally handicapped are referred to without question as patients and medical rather than educational treatment is given priority.

The increasing medical domination of the field is also reflected in the post-war incorporation of asylums into the National Health Service, as subnormality hospitals – without any public debate as to whether they should be or not. This move served to create a split between the centrally financed administration of the hospitals and the locally financed community and education services. It is a split which has heightened the isolation of the hospitals from the communities they are supposed to serve and which has left them stagnating with insufficient staff, resources or finance.

That scientific theories rather than moral or religious explanations of mental handicap have come to dominate the field does not therefore mean that other perspectives have disappeared. Medical and psychological knowledge all too frequently fails to provide what many parents and many handicapped people need to make sense of their lives, even supposing they, like medical staff, were to have access to such information. They ask the question, 'Why should this happen to me?', even where there is a clear medical diagnosis. Some parents may still see their handicapped child as the consequence of a misdeed or misfortune of their own or even as a blessing in disguise from God, sent to test their faith and fortitude.

A handicapped child can embody all a woman's secret fears about her inability to reproduce life, or her fantasies about her own 'wrongness' – feelings which many women who do not bear handicapped children can also experience.[80] It is, in many instances, women who do bear the burden of this fear and guilt, a reflection of the fact that women have also received a disproportionate share of the social blame for producing defective children.

The play *A Day in the Death of Joe Egg* illustrates the needs and despair of parents very clearly:

Sheila [the wife]: Well, of course you find out gradually, not all at once, but there is a point where you finally accept it. And that's . . . Oh, very nasty, you think 'Why me?' I don't know about the other mothers, but I kept saying 'Why me, why me?' all day long. Then you get tired of that and you say 'Why not me?'

And later:

Sheila: When you're up against a – disaster of this kind – it's so numbing that you must make some sense of it – otherwise – you'd –
Brian: Give up hope?
Sheila: My husband doesn't need to make sense of anything. He lives with despair.[81]

In blaming herself for their handicapped child, the wife Sheila actually mentions her promiscuity before marriage. She also says how she felt she was holding the baby back during a long labour: this she sees as a subconscious shrinking from motherhood. The husband on the other hand blames the doctors for having 'botched' it, a typical male/female difference that maybe allows the husband in the end to kill the child without guilt.

Contemporary science – biology, medicine, psychology – does not explicitly concern itself with how mentally handicapped people can strain our sense of what is human, nor with the extent of their exclusion from society. Professional training ensures that doctors, nurses and teachers need not ask these questions either. But the absence of such questions from the professional and scientific literature does not mean they have ceased to be important. They live on in the despair of parents, and, as we have seen, in the life of the ward. They emerge as burning issues in the lives of mentally handicapped people, in their struggles to gain some self-respect and independence – and in the inquiries of recent years into the mental handicap services and the inadequacies these have revealed.

Chapter 6

Old Ideologies for New

Public attention was brought to bear on conditions in mental handicap hospitals in 1967 and 1968 through two newspaper articles.[1] What is significant about this is the silence that existed previously, and the extreme difficulty of making anything public. The nursing assistant who made the initial allegations about Ely Hospital to the *News of the World* had previously been threatened by a senior hospital official that his life would be made unpleasant if he made an official complaint. And the article in the *Guardian* about Harperbury Hospital provoked a storm of defensive reactions from the hospital management as well as a reprimand from the Press Council. Crossman (then Minister of Health) records in his diary that civil servants in the Ministry knew four years previously what conditions in Ely and other hospitals were like, but did not pass on the information, either within the Civil Service or to the regional hospital boards concerned.[2] He also describes the attempts of civil servants and medical officers to prevent the full publication of the subsequent Ely report, and the resulting delay in its appearance.

Better Services for the Mentally Handicapped, a government policy document published in 1971, in response to these and other exposures, set the framework for much of the ensuing debate and criticism about hospitals. Committing itself to the principle that mentally handicapped people shouldn't be 'unnecessarily' segregated from other people, it envisaged a reduction by half in hospital places by 1991, and a corresponding increase in local authority funded care – hostels, day centres, boarding out. At the same time it promised upgrading of existing hospitals, and advocated an end to old custodial methods and attitudes. Whilst recommending the re-education and increased training of hospital staff, it never queried whether hospitals were the right place for any mentally handicapped people. Subsequent government circulars specified minimum standards of space, personal clothing and staffing ratios for hospitals.

Since then life in mental subnormality hospitals has been investigated more and more thoroughly in a series of official inquiries and research studies, much of the detail of which has been used in previous chapters of this book. The last decade has certainly been one of upheaval and uncertainty for the hospitals; much of the debate has been about whether mentally handicapped people should be in hospital at all, and whether people with nursing training are the most suitable to look after them. In 1979, the Jay report recommended the end of the dual system of hospital and local care, with a transfer to the latter, and a social work, rather than a nursing, training for the staff of all residential care units.[3] It remains to be seen how much of this is put into practice.

What kind of changes then has this last decade seen? And how do these changes relate to the issues of the past that were discussed in the last chapter?

MODERN STANDARDS OF CARE

The available evidence suggests that only for a small minority of mentally handicapped people has life changed significantly. The population of long-stay hospitals has fallen, but not to the extent envisaged by the planners of *Better Services*. Much of this fall is due to a restriction in the admission of children, and a relatively high death rate in an increasingly ageing population. Although discharges have increased, so too have admissions over all – resulting in a greater use of hospitals for short-term care. Local authority provision of hostels and training centres for adults has expanded but again more slowly than expected.[4] Despite the sizeable decrease in the number of children in mental handicap hospitals, there has been no equivalent expansion in local authority residential places for them at all – presumably these children are being looked after at home.[5] Over all the proportion of NHS capital expenditure spent on mental handicap services dropped between

1970 and 1975 despite various commitments to make them (along with other non-acute services) a priority.[6]

The appalling physical and material conditions, and the chronic understaffing of particular hospitals have continued to receive brief national publicity. The inquiry into Normansfield Hospital, for example, revealed that many of the same problems existed in 1977 as had been described several years previously in other hospitals. No cruelty was found, but standards of nursing care were described as 'generally extremely low'.[7] The buildings were in a decrepit, often dangerous, state of repair, and urine and faeces were at times left unattended for days. In 1978, a year after the initial visits, conditions were no better. Once again, it was those who were officially responsible for the hospital – the Area Health Authority – who were aware of the conditions and the tyranny of the particular consultant, but who did almost nothing about it. It is outsiders, the local community health council, and a teacher in the hospital school, who are praised for persisting with their attempts to expose and publicize the situation at Normansfield.

A report on Tatchbury Mount Hospital in Wessex, where there have been many innovative schemes put into practice, showed how despite a relatively favourable staff–patient ratio the nurses still saw their roles as primarily custodial and body-servicing.[8] The report found a low level of personal care, scruffy and inadequate clothing, and very poor communication between the staff, especially at senior levels.

Conditions in Leavesden Hospital in 1978 sometimes reached the point where

... staffing is not the only shortage in the hospital. Food is another. At one point we were unable to get cornflakes from the store for three weeks. During this time, for a period of two days, no oats were available with which to make porridge. On several occasions there have been no fats in store and on other days no bacon, no biscuits, no fruit. Clothing is another thing in short supply. Several times I have been told that no vests or pants are in stock. For several weeks there were no men's socks. Domestic staff is also very short – some weekends some wards are not covered at all by domestic staff, thus throwing more work on to the shoulders of long-suffering nurses.[9]

And the report of the National Development Group showed what a high proportion of hospitals had not, in 1975, reached the minimum standards laid down in 1969.[10] It notes how the DHSS has done very little to ensure that hospitals implement its recommendations, and how frequently new ideas are met by inertia within the hospitals. It sees the lack of accountability of hospitals to its residents, their families, or the public, as one of the factors contributing to this inertia, and also criticizes hospital management for not stimulating 'inactive' staff.

In 1978 two further research studies were also published concerning hospital and other forms of residential care. These provide a revealing degree of detail about the everyday life of mentally handicapped people.

Maureen Oswin's study surveyed life in wards for multiply handicapped children in eight different hospitals.[11] She describes what is by now an all too familiar picture: understaffing, inadequate resources, poor standards of hygiene and physical care. She also found a marked lack of specialist services for these children – dental care, physiotherapy, speech training – services which for many are the rationale of large hospitals.

The social isolation of these children was often extreme. Contact between them and the staff was minimal: in every ten hours the children received one hour of physical care (washing, feeding, dressing, toileting, etc.), and only *five minutes* of so-called 'mothering' attention (playing, cuddling, talking to, etc.). Contact between the children was seldom actively encouraged – as it needs to be if it is to happen at all – and it was often actually prevented by the domestic routines or unthinking behaviour of the staff. Kindly and conscientious though the staff often were, they were frequently pessimistic and unimaginative about doing anything other than looking after the children physically, keeping them quiet, clean, and no trouble to anyone. For such children, life can only be described as one of multiple deprivation, exacerbating their already existing multiple handicap.

The second study, published by Campaign for Mentally Handicapped, is especially interesting in that it contains the first attempt to specify the different needs of mentally handicapped people and to follow this up by assessing the extent to which these are met by different forms of care.[12] It examines hospital wards, hospital annexes, hostels, group homes, and lodgings over one entire NHS region. It looks at these services not from a professional or administrative point of view, but in terms of the quality of life of the recipients of these services. The author, Tyne, found that the larger-sized units, in particular the hospitals, often failed to provide adequately for even the most basic needs like food, warmth, clothing, sanitation. Despite official upgrading, the hospital wards often had minimal material resources; they always failed to provide for other personal and emotional needs (for example, sustained relationships, privacy, occupation, leisure) and personal growth (education, training).

One of the main conclusions of this study is that although now '. . . buildings are brighter and breezier', most of the changes since 1968 have been relatively superficial:

The fundamental problems in the organization and funding of our services still remain, and fundamental ideologies about institutions still have not been seriously rethought. For these reasons, some of the most wretched problems still remain and seem likely to continue into the future.

The last decade has also seen the formation of new pressure groups, more militant and challenging than the long established charities. Small self-help groups of parents have appeared, highly critical not just of the lack of adequate provision to children's needs, but also of the attitudes of the various professionals.[13] The lack of interest and relevant expertise of doctors is recorded again and again, as is the frequently patronizing attitude of other professionals, psychologists and social workers especially, towards parents. In one rare instance parents have succeeded in obtaining what they wanted from the local authority – a small local house where their severely handicapped children could be looked after as part of the neighbourhood, rather than dispersed to hospitals twenty-five or more miles away.[14] CMH, the Campaign for the Mentally Handicapped, has also grown steadily since its foundation in 1971. It has involved mentally handicapped people in workshops and conferences designed not just to find out what mentally handicapped people want for themselves, but also to give them and the various professionals involved a chance to meet each other on more neutral and equal territory. It has also produced a series of inquiries and reports on all areas of life affecting mentally handicapped people, as well as radically criticizing government policies.

In the last ten years also the hospital and other workers have begun to organize themselves on a wider scale. Many more nursing staff and ancillary staff have joined unions (as is the case within the whole NHS) and other professional workers have started their own association. A new specialist journal of mental subnormality nursing (*Apex*) has appeared, and an Institute of Mental Subnormality, based in a hospital and mainly concerned with hospital issues, has been formed. These initiatives reflect a growing concern amongst nurses and associated staff about their professional standing – their skills and knowledge, as well as their status and pay.

Running through the debates of the last ten years there has been a significant change in some of the ideologies and concepts of mental handicap. The historic concern with the human status of the mentally handicapped has become a concern with their normality – or at any rate how normal they can be made. The older question 'How human?' and the modern question 'How normal?' mean essentially the same: 'How like us, the rest of humanity, are they?' Linked to the desire for change in the conditions of life of so many mentally handicapped people, there has been a renewal of the old ideology of optimism about them. Many current proposals for reform within the subnormality services and institutions are based upon the assumption that mentally handicapped people can lead a more normal life than was previously thought, or that they can be educated and trained to do so.

At the core of the government proposals of 1971 is the argument that old custodial practices are no longer appropriate '*because* (my italics) of the work done to show that even the severely subnormal can develop skills if trained.'[15] It is not just that changed facilities and methods of care are likely to lead to a greater development of an individual's abilities and satisfactions, but that the expenditure of human and financial resources is *justified* as worthwhile in terms of either this outcome or its possibility.

RECENT PSYCHOLOGICAL RESEARCH

The source of renewed optimism about mentally handicapped people's abilities appears to be the ideas and discoveries of experimental psychology. The last two decades have seen a slow growth of professional and academic interest in mental handicap and there have been many psychological investigations of how the mentally handicapped learn. This emphasis on learning is a reflection of psychology's preoccupation in general with cognitive processes, as well as the domination of the IQ definition of mental handicap: for many psychologists, IQ and learning ability are equated. The fruits of this extensive research have been summed up as follows: 'At least one conclusion emerges with absolute clarity from twenty years of experimental work: any human being, of whatever level, is capable of at least some learning.'[16]

This conclusion may not seem to need twenty years' empirical work to prove it. Strictly speaking it may not even be true – there are people in various conditions such as extreme brain damage whose only possible change is deterioration. But it is a statement which is extremely important as an expression of basic belief and from it follow all kinds of attitudes and activities. The belief is strikingly similar to the Victorian one – that all idiots are capable of some improvement – which underlay Seguin's methods of instruction and the efforts of other educationalists of that time.

It has taken until the second half of this century for psychologists to discover much of what was already known fifty years earlier and had simply been socially repressed – namely, that mentally handicapped people can display all kinds of skills if the conditions for acquiring and using them are appropriate. Thus the finding in the early 'fifties that mentally handicapped people could do simple industrial-type tasks if given adequate time to learn them was regarded as a major discovery.[17] It has also been found that an individual's final level of achievement on a task of this kind is not predictable from his or her starting level – i.e. that conditions of teaching and learning can make a lot of difference to behaviour that was once thought of as unchangeable and inherent.[18]

Psychologists have often written about the supposed characteristics of mentally handicapped people exclusively in terms of *their* defects and limitations, and not sufficiently in terms of the environments they have been exposed to. Much of their behaviour does no more than reflect our expectations of them, and the inadequacy of the life to which they are subjected. Yet many psychological generalizations have been made about them (or their essential nature), completely ignoring the fact that the people concerned had often spent a whole lifetime in the highly depriving environment of the mental handicap hospital.[19] It seems to require a radical shift in thinking to see the behaviour of mentally handicapped people in terms of their experience of life – a shift which many of those most closely involved with them, as well as experimental psychologists, find very difficult to make.

Research into learning has also produced many comparisons between handicapped and non-handicapped people. A significant conclusion of some of this research is that the processes of learning of these two groups differ in degree rather than in kind, and that the strategies and methods of thought are essentially the same.[20] From this it has been inferred that people of any IQ level are governed by the same 'laws' of behaviour. These findings have been challenged by Jensen, in experiments designed to show that there are fundamental differences between people according to their IQ scores and thus support his contention that IQ has a very high genetic component.[21] He proposes subnormal and normal types of learning, using this distinction to argue for a different and much more limited form of education for those with lower IQ scores.

The argument within psychology, about whether there is a qualitative or a quantitative difference between handicapped and non-handicapped people, is not, fundamentally, one to be settled by empirical evidence, although it takes this form because of the obsessively scientific nature of psychology. Evidence can be produced to support either position, or neither, depending on the conditions of the experiment, the exact kind of behaviour investigated and the methods and interests of the researcher. What is more important is the way in which this debate within psychology reflects a wider social debate on the inclusion or exclusion of mentally handicapped people from so many social institutions. Unfortunately, this reflection is not always a conscious process as far as the psychologists themselves are concerned.

One of the most important and consistent differences that has been found concerns speed of learning and responding.[22] Relative slowness is something that handicaps many people – a consequence of the fact that we live in a society where time is quite literally money, where the demands of competitive industrialized production mean faster and faster work speeds. Time, as Marx said, 'is the room of human development'.[23] Mentally handicapped people are disadvantaged not only because much of their current behaviour is too slow by prevailing standards, but also because their rate of development as children is slower than the norm. The IQ score is after all no more than an expression of comparative progress up a normative scale of behaviour measured in terms of time taken (mental age divided by chronological age) to achieve a certain level. The mentally handicapped are those who take the longest time to get to a certain point – the ultimate definition and reduction of them in terms of speed – although this is not how psychologists would describe what the IQ measures.[24]

Mentally handicapped people are also less able than most to learn spontaneously from ordinary life experiences, and need more carefully planned instruction.[25] Again, this observation, made as long ago as 1866, seems to have had to be rediscovered recently.[26] It underlines the overriding importance of the environment. Mentally handicapped people are far more vulnerable to the depressing and depriving effect of barren surroundings since they are much less able to create their own stimulation and goals. Yet more than any other group of people they are still exposed to such environments, only to thereby fulfil the expectation that they are 'hopeless', not 'worth the time'.[27]

A crude environmentalism based on the work of the American psychologist B. F. Skinner has also become popular. The assumptions of this approach, as applied to the mentally handicapped, are that anybody's behaviour can be 'modified' (i.e. changed) if the required behaviour is broken down into sufficiently discrete units and if the correct system of rewards is used at each stage of learning. Since no pre-existing level of functioning or understanding is required, behaviour modification methods are especially suitable for the severely handicapped, those with a minimal level of response or without language.

This approach requires a close scrutiny of the immediate environment to see how undesirable behaviour (defined as such by nurses or psychologists) is maintained by other people's responses to it. Nurses, for example, have come to realize that inadvertently they often give a patient their attention for troublesome behaviour and not for less disruptive 'good' behaviour.[28] In the ward, where a situation of scarcity prevails, attempts to eliminate undesirable behaviour by conventional means such as scolding are bound to fail, since such behaviour is effectively rewarded by the unusual contact and attention that it elicits.

Behaviourist approaches have been implemented in many practical training programmes, especially in hospitals. The pages of nursing journals are now full of reports of behaviour modification experiments and 'token economy' reward systems. Courses are increasingly offered to nurses for training in the principles and methods involved. Behaviour modification is often hailed as the means by which radical reform of the hospital can be affected now that there is, according to one commentator, 'a real possibility of major change in behaviours that were unalterable.'[29]

Is it possible to say that behaviour modification works? There is no simple answer to the question. It is certainly true that changes in behaviour have been produced that no one previously thought possible – in toilet training and self-feeding, for example.[30] Such improvements in self-care are not only desirable as ends in themselves but also seem to generate other beneficial consequences, such as more activity and independence in other areas of life, or more easily run wards. Yet often a behaviour modification programme may be the only one to have been tried for years, seldom with any comparison to other methods of learning. The failures that are reported are seldom analysed in terms of the learning methods employed, or the characteristics of the individuals involved; they may be due to problems of implementing programmes in a ward setting, of maintaining behaviour once the rewards have been discontinued, or of transferring individuals back to the ward from the experimental context.[31]

Although there has initially been some resistance in England to the introduction of behaviour modification methods, this seems to have evaporated in the enthusiasm for what can be achieved and for the new roles it allows nurses and psychologists to adopt. The doubts and criticisms do, however, remain. It is an extremely powerful method of controlling behaviour, especially that of someone who does not fully understand what he or she is being subjected to. No choice is given on participation in programmes, nor on what aspects of behaviour are to be altered, nor on the kinds of reward used.

As for definitions of 'desirable' or 'undesirable' behaviour, these are entirely up to the staff of the hospital and so inevitably reflect their priorities rather than those of the patients. Increased independence in dressing, for example, may be an advantage to the staff of a ward. But for the handicapped person it may represent a loss of much desired human and bodily contact which is not replaced in any other way. Token economy systems (in which patients have to reach a specified standard on daily tasks before earning their tokens which then can be exchanged for cash or goods) can be extremely coercive; leisure activities such as watching television or lying on the bed in the day time which, it might be thought, anyone has a right to, are used as rewards and withheld unless the required behaviour is forthcoming.[32]

As a result of psychological interest generally, a more developmental approach to mentally handicapped people is emerging, an acknowledgement that a process of growth, however slight and slow, is going on, a process that is highly susceptible to environmental encouragement or discouragement. The aims of care and training are now frequently expressed in terms of 'develop to maximum potential' or 'full exploitation of potential'. For many people the application in schools and hospitals of the discoveries of psychology appears to promise a better future. The focus, nevertheless, is still very much on changing the behaviour of each mentally handicapped individual; the behaviour of others (except in as far as they are to carry out an instructional programme), or the effects of the total environment, are seldom investigated. And because most psychological approaches do not have a sufficiently comprehensive view of what it is like to live one's life as a mentally handicapped person, or to work as a nurse in a mental subnormality hospital, the measure of success hoped for does not always materialize. Enthusiasm for new ideas often fails to survive the reality of trying to implement them in an adverse and isolated situation. It is often the younger newly-trained staff who express the view that little can be done '. . . except feed and water them . . . all that stuff they teach you in training school – they ought to come out here and try it.'[33]

CONCEPTS OF NORMALIZATION

From quite different sources an ideology of 'normalization' has become current, emphasizing the importance of the total environment and how institutional environments particularly contribute greatly to the burden of being handicapped. The so-called 'normalization principle' has become the guiding philosophy of those who argue that mentally handicapped people should not live in hospitals of any kind. This principle would, according to one of its leading Scandinavian proponents, make available to all mentally handicapped people '. . . patterns of life and conditions of everyday living which are as close as possible to the regular circumstances and ways of life of society'.[34] Similarly, CMH argues that the aim of services for mentally handicapped should be to enable them to lead 'as normal a life as possible'.[35] This includes a normal rhythm of days, weeks and years, normal-sized living units, adequate privacy, normal access to social, emotional and sexual relationships with others, normal growing-up experiences, the possibility of decently paid work, choice and participation in decisions affecting their future.

The needs of mentally handicapped people are seen as basically similar to those of ordinary people, with the difference that they may not be able to meet these needs unaided or as independently as other people can, and that they may have additional special needs, such as specific medical or therapeutic requirements.[36] It is argued that these additional needs do not mean that mentally handicapped people have to live separately from others, or that the special services they need must be provided in the place where they live (as in hospital) but could be met through the general medical and social services, as are other people's special requirements.

'Normalization' can mean many different things to different people and it has other advocates who see it as quite compatible with a sufficiently reformed hospital life. Doctors and psychologists arguing for changes within the hospital system often adopt such a position. Thus, Gunzburg, an influential advocate of moderate change, propounds the idea of the hospital as a normalizing environment: 'An intensive training environment which whilst not normal in itself will nevertheless help to normalize people.'[37] He sees the mentally handicapped as having 'deficiencies in living skills'. In providing them with 'normal living experiences', both formally and informally, the hospital should enable them to practise 'normal skills of living' and thus become more acceptable outside.

Another advocate of hospital reform, Day, says: 'Normalization of the physical environment is essential to a personalized approach to care and a normal living routine, and it is now accepted that residents of all ability levels should live in small groups in a substitute home environment.'[38] Behind this approach to the physical environment lies the philosophy that 'treating the mentally handicapped person as an individual is a most important aspect of the normal approach to care' – an acknowledgement that to date the mentally handicapped have not been treated as individuals. Day sees this normalization being achieved not just by a much greater flexibility of ward regimes, but also by the increased development of mentally handicapped people as the consumers of goods and leisure activities – clothing and television, for instance – an idea which crudely encapsulates contemporary notions of the value and functioning of the individual in society.

A similar commitment to a normal lifestyle 'within the community' is one of the principles on which the recent Jay report is based, the other principles being their right to be treated as individuals, and their right to obtain additional help from the community in which they live and from professional services.[39] From these principles come the recommendations for a flexible system of small group living, and an end to the domination of nursing care.

These views of 'normalization' entail a much greater degree of integration of mentally handicapped people with the rest of society than exists now. From such a standpoint life in a hospital can never be normal.

In examining the arguments for extensive normalization of the lives of mentally handicapped people, it can be seen that the common basis is a claim to humanity which they share with the non-handicapped. Nirje, for example, states as part of his argument for the 'normalization principle' that 'A person is a person first, the handicap is secondary.'[40] Another advocate of normalization maintains '. . . these are ordinary people who must have rights and duties similar to those of every other citizen.'[41] And a popular pamphlet published by C M H and Mind claims:

The important thing is that mentally handicapped people are *people*. Everyone enjoys being with friends and joining in what's going on as far as they can. Everyone gets sad and bored and angry if they feel alone. Mentally handicapped people don't feel any differently just because their brains learn more slowly.[42]

Statements such as these are conspicuously missing from the proposals of various professional-interest groups, such as doctors and nurses, who tend to see mentally handicapped people much more in terms of their abnormalities and needs for special services. It is true that the normalization arguments run a risk of idealizing the common humanity which, it is claimed, exists between mentally handicapped people and the rest of society. Insufficient attention is paid to the difficulty of recognizing, valuing and sharing this common humanity. However, it is not the case, as some critics argue, that these arguments deny the existence of any handicap at all; the C M H proposals, for example, demonstrate a full understanding of the special problems that mentally handicapped people may encounter and of particular kinds of help and treatment they may need (for example, assistance with money for those earning wages, help with choices, wheel-chair access to buildings, support in confronting a difficult and hostile world, special technical aids, advice about relationships).

RIGHTS TO NORMALITY

A frequent claim made by those arguing for various forms of 'normalization' is that mentally handicapped people have a *right* to normality. Given the degree of exclusion from society that mentally handicapped people have suffered, the abnormality that has been forced upon them, gaining this right in a concrete way, would be a momentous achievement, and one which we are very far from achieving. However, 'normalization' and the 'right to normality' cannot be accepted uncritically. Such arguments often have a very unquestioning attitude to the normality that is proclaimed as a right. Conventional and conformist lifestyles can be imposed on mentally handicapped people in the name of normality, standards that are almost an exaggeration of normality. Thus 'normalization' within the hospital is often seen as recreating the family: 'Residents are encouraged to undertake the roles they would have in a normal family, the women doing the domestic chores and assisting in the day-to-day care of the children and the men going out to work.'[43]

Normalization can mean much greater pressure on mentally handicapped people to adjust to prevailing customs and standards. Nirje describes it as involving a 'better adjustment to society'. It does not necessarily mean that 'normality' will adjust to fit them. Many of the normalization arguments are very humane, in the sense that by the standards of the immediate past, they propose a great amelioration in the conditions of life for many handicapped people. What they seldom do, however, is raise the question of how we, the normal society into which mentally handicapped people are supposed to become more integrated, are likely to respond to this, or what changes are going to be demanded of us. The normalization proposals simply suppose that as mentally handicapped people become more normal, or their lives resemble those of most other people more, they will be more acceptable and accepted. There is a very real basis for this supposition: sub-human living conditions make the people in them seem sub-human too, but the full implications of these proposals are seldom followed through. It is often left to those who are most hostile to the ideas of 'normalization' to question whether the 'community' is willing to accept more mentally handicapped people amongst them or to do more than passively tolerate them.

The assertion that mentally handicapped people should have equal rights with all other citizens often has a hollow ring to it. The UN declaration of the rights of mentally handicapped people, which includes their right to special services and adequate care and treatment, simply poses the question: who is going to implement these rights and how? There is always a danger with equal rights' arguments that existing material, psychological and cultural inequalities are overlooked. (For example, a right to equal pay for women is of little concrete benefit if there are no available jobs, or no adequate provision for child-care so that women could actually work at such jobs.) With mentally handicapped people, we have to ensure that they are actually able to use any improved opportunities that they are presented with. If, for example, their right to ordinary housing is accepted, if they are provided with ordinary houses and flats to live in, we also have to ensure that there is adequate human and social support for them to do so. If we try to make available a wider range of life-experiences for them, a greater degree of choice of occupation, of friends, of leisure activities, we have to ensure that these experiences are not overwhelmingly negative for them, that they are not teased, ignored or badly treated at work, on the street, in public places. Implementation of such rights would make great demands on the attitudes and responses of the increased number of people who would, either voluntarily or accidentally, come into contact with mentally handicapped people.

The implementation of these rights for mentally handicapped people would undoubtedly require more money being spent on them. This question of financial cost is one which many reforming groups have often dodged; some have even tried to prove that their proposals would not cost any more than present arrangements. Others have argued that within the terms of welfare economics, increased investment in the training of mentally handicapped people would bring long-term economic benefits from the wages they would eventually earn and their contribution to the total economy thereby.[44] It is not surprising that people engage in such cost-effectiveness arguments, particularly in an era of cuts in social welfare spending.

Whilst mental handicap services were made a relative priority within the NHS in 1975, a recent statement by the Minister responsible, in an introduction to the NDG report on hospitals, is hardly encouraging: he will support any changes that do not cost money.[45] The Jay report tackles this issue head on: their proposals would undoubtedly cost more in the short term, since they require a doubling in the number of staff needed. They argue that increased spending is essential if there is to be any radical change at all, and that we should make a commitment at the level of national priorities to this. Despite the figures provided by this and other reports, they cannot be taken at face value as representing the actual cost of implementing the various proposals. They do not take into account any long-term economic benefits that might come from the much greater participation of mentally handicapped people in the life of the nation, and the savings in costs made by, for example, providing adequate domiciliary support to the many families who now have to hospitalize their children for lack of any other alternative. And models that might take these consequences into account (like similar models of the economics of education) are notorious for the large number of untestable assumptions that have to be built into them. None of these considerations, however, avoid the moral question of what as a society our priorities are in respect of mentally handicapped people.

These arguments also assume that mentally handicapped people will accept the normalization of their lives. There is little doubt, judging from the expressed opinions of the people that have been asked, that they would welcome a lessening of the enforced abnormalities and deprivations in their lives, and a chance to experience at least some of the choices that most ordinary people take for granted. However, we also have to allow for the possibility that mentally handicapped people may wish to question and reject some of the more exploitative and oppressive standards of our society, just as many non-handicapped people do. Many people choose to live in various unconventional ways, for example, in communes in the country, or shared households in the city, to reject certain standards of conventional dress and typical sex-role behaviour, and mentally handicapped people may wish to do so too. If the 'right to normality' is not to become a whole series of pressures on mentally handicapped people to change and conform to other people's standards, then this right must include both the right and the means to question that normality, and to live a different life, one that is an enrichment rather than a deprivation of 'normality'.

Chapter 7

Which Way is Forward?

Our current social philosophies about mentally handicapped people, and the arguments about their future, tend to be expressed in terms of state welfare provision: the type of service they are thought to need, and the professions required to administer and deliver these services. The terms of these arguments simply reflect the fact that most of their lives are administered and financed through the state welfare system in one form or another – NHS, social service departments, local education authorities, etc. Most of the people who care for or educate them are also state employees, and arguments on the part of those involved in the care of the mentally handicapped tend to reflect their status as professionals or semi-professionals within the welfare state.

PROFESSIONAL POLITICS

It is no accident that those with the most vested interest in the continuation of the existing large institutions, or of the primacy of the nursing and medical professions, should also be those who most emphasize the sub- and ab-normality of mentally handicapped people. Their whole careers have been based on the non-normality of their charges, on the rejection of mentally handicapped people by society outside the hospital. Thus, the Royal College of Psychiatrists refers to the supposedly 'unaesthetic' behaviour of mentally handicapped people as an argument for the 'privacy' and 'space' that hospitals allegedly provide.[1] One doctor sees hospitals as 'a tolerant enclave in an intolerant world', the only place in which 'intractable problems' can be managed.[2] Another consultant, an ardent defender of the hospitals, criticizes

CMH for its alleged 'misunderstanding' that the mentally handicapped are normal and should be treated as such.[3] And yet another, in arguing for the continuation of large specialized 'communities' and against a decentralized local service, finds it necessary to affirm that 'the mentally handicapped *are* mentally handicapped', as though this were being denied.[4]

Criticizing what they call the 'emasculated humanitarianism' of the advocates of normalization, two nurses clearly state that the imposition of normal environmental demands is not the function of a subnormality hospital.[5] What the hospital should provide instead is an environment in which people who have been rejected by the normal world can cope and progress. While other nurses may not reject so explicitly all the criteria of normality, at the same time they seldom question the abnormality of the hospital environment or the many ways in which they do define their charges as quite different from themselves, as previous chapters have shown. Most nursing textbooks teach that the mentally handicapped are not normal, and never will be, and medical textbooks refer to them entirely in terms of their known or suspected pathologies.

The argument about the future of hospitals is also carried out in inter-professional terms: which profession – nursing, medical, social work, educational, or psychological – should have major control over the lives of the mentally handicapped? There is much talk about the need for inter- or multi-disciplinary teams. Some of this, particularly the suggestion that a special mental handicap service and profession (and even Minister) should be created, reflects the frustration of those having to deal with the present fragmented system of care, where bureaucratic procedures and inter-professional rivalry and non-cooperation often prevent what resources there are being used as effectively as possible.[6] But it also reflects the desires of those who would have their careers assured through such a unified specialist service, and their fears for themselves if mentally handicapped people were to get more of their needs met through the same ordinary services as other people.

The staff of hospitals, since the initial Ely exposures, have fought first a defensive and now an increasingly offensive battle to ensure the future of hospitals, their jobs and status. One consultant

sees the 1960s as the 'decade of the attack upon mental subnormality hospitals'.[7] 1968 and 1969 were 'particularly sad years for
the staffs of mental subnormality hospitals'. He does not mention
the many sad (or worse) years that thousands of patients have
spent in the same hospitals. The South Ockendon inquiry found
that the abuse of 'clinical freedom' by some doctors, and the lack
of any challenge to the decisions of individual consultants, led to
some particularly bad experiences for some of the patients.[8] This
is seen as 'unfair' by the same doctor, because the report did not
understand the position of the superintendent, 'whose authority
was insidiously eroded' by the recent abolition of one-person rule
in favour of a tripartite management structure.[9] Hospital multi-
disciplinary teams can now 'over-rule' consultants, leading to 'loss
of morale'.

The 1974 reorganization of the NHS, which resulted in decision-
taking being more remote from each hospital and often subject to
non-specialist influence, is seen by another consultant as meaning
that Area Health Authority planning teams are really 'plotting
teams', conspiring with the DHSS to dissolve the hospitals.[10]
Multi-disciplinary teams which the doctors are having to accept
are only welcomed on the basis that it is the medical personnel
who will retain essential control of the other professions. As the
Royal College of Psychiatrists pronounced '. . . the clinician must
remain the coordinator of the clinical team to ensure that "training" principles do not take precedence over medical needs . . . no
hospital . . . can be run non-medically.'[11] Of the consultant:
'There are no areas in the management of patients in hospital that
do not ultimately come under his aegis.'[12]

Arguments for retaining patients in hospital are put in terms of
the lack of any 'hard scientific evidence' that they are better off
outside, completely ignoring all the different living situations, or
the desires of the mentally handicapped people themselves.[13] The
only point at which the possible needs of patients are considered
is when some of the advantages of hospitals are cited: the protection from a hostile and indifferent world, the range of social life
and entertainment provided in some hospitals, the choice of com-
panions and lack of isolation for some patients.

Some of these statements may sound like the last rattlings of a few dead-wood consultants failing to face up to the changes that are happening. They certainly do not represent the views of many doctors who would welcome far-reaching changes within the hospitals. However, it is important not to underestimate the power of the medical profession to resist any changes which would mean a diminution in their power, or to take control of any changes that are made.

Crossman records how at the time of the Ely report there was great resistance within the medical profession as a whole to the proposal to switch a greater proportion of health service money into subnormality hospitals.[14] The idea of an independent inspectorate (the Hospital Advisory Service) was strongly resisted by both the medical profession and the civil servants, and after a few years this was changed into the National Development Team with much weaker powers of inspection. We have already seen how the response of some doctors to having their absolute power as superintendents challenged by the advent of multi-disciplinary management teams is to try to take control of these teams. In general, the medical profession has been very self-seeking in its response to the growth of other professions in the field, and to the increasing questioning of the role of medical specialists in mental handicap hospitals. The debate has been carried on almost entirely within the profession, and they have demanded developments such as the creation of a 'cadre' élite of doctors, additional training, academic and research posts.[15]

Recently a hospital action group led by a doctor has been formed, to publicize the advantages of hospital life and to counter what they regard as the constant adverse negative publicity.[16] Believing that hospitals can provide the best kind of home for mentally handicapped people, if not starved of resources, they also emphasize the advantages of size: the wide range of professional skills and specialist services, the leisure facilities and social life. They suggest that hospitals should increasingly concentrate on the most severely handicapped, who are seen as incapable of living elsewhere; the mildly handicapped they would like to see 'in the community', an echo of the old distinction between the pathological (medical) and the sub-cultural (non-medical) groups, described in Chapter 5. This reservation of hospital life for only the severely handicapped is becoming an increasingly common assumption (or fall-back position) as more hostel provision is made. This is despite the fact that severely handicapped people suffer at least as much, if not more, as the mildly handicapped from the nature of hospital life. Oswin's study, for example, shows how the depriving nature of their environment depressed the limited abilities of the multiply handicapped children even further, unable as they were to create any kind of stimulation or social contact for themselves.[17] The findings of the Wessex experiments, with mixed-ability hostels, and the recommendations of the Jay report, refute the suggestion that it is impossible for the severely and multiply handicapped to live outside hospital, though clearly additional resources are needed to enable them to do so.[18]

PROFESSIONAL POLITICS – NURSES

The writings and speeches of the nurses (or their representatives) reflect clearly the sense that they have been scapegoated for the much criticized state of the hospitals. Press reports, sociological surveys, and proposals for radical change are felt as 'knocking the hospital' and 'blaming the nurses', however often it is emphasized that it is the whole system that is at fault, rather than the individual nurses, whose dedication and hard work are frequently praised. The Normansfield inquiry, for example, is seen as a 'punch in the face' for nurses, despite the fact that its strongest indictment was not of the nurses but of the Area Health Authority, the hospital management and the consultant.[19] It is of course very easy to focus on the behaviour and attitudes of the nurses, because they are the most evident link between the whole system of the hospital and the recipients of care, the patients. They are the people who are in continual contact with the people the hospital is supposed to be serving, they mediate all the routines, plans, objectives, that other professionals devise and administer.

Proposals to lessen the numbers of people in hospital, for a gradual evolution towards care 'in the community', and suggestions that most mentally handicapped people do not need specifically nursing care, are met by replies such as 'nurses are the experts' or seen as a 'threat to a profession'.[20] On the one hand the nurses complain that the inquiries and government committees set up to look into the future of subnormality hospitals have created an atmosphere of uncertainty about their jobs, a loss of morale within the hospitals, and a general passing of responsibility from one quarter to another. On the other hand, the nursing organizations have taken the opportunity opened up by the events of the last ten years to demand a higher professional status, better pay and training, a higher proportion of qualified nurses.

The Briggs report (on nursing in general) proposed in 1974 that mental subnormality nurses should eventually be replaced by a different kind of profession, with a less medical orientation and a predominantly child-care or residential social work training. Other organizations, notably Mind and NSMHC, have taken up this idea, suggesting a 'new caring profession' as has the Jay report. For the most part, nurses have responded extremely defensively to this idea, seeing only the threat to their present profession, and not, for the most, part looking at the other issues involved, about the kind of life that is desired by many mentally handicapped people.[21] The nurses are not alone in displaying such clearly self-interested behaviour – the doctors have been just as concerned to preserve their roles and jobs. No criticism is intended here of the struggles of nurses to obtain better conditions of pay and work, and to not be exploited for their sense of duty and dedication towards the patients. This is a demand that all workers need constantly to make of their employers if they are not to accept a falling standard of living. But there is an important difference between a militant refusal to accept low wages, long hours, and inadequate training for the job, on the one hand, and on the other, a defensive insistence on job demarcation, an unwillingness to look at the needs of the patients in any other than a traditional light, or to acknowledge that the system they are caught up in may need fundamental changes. This lack of critical reflection on the part of nurses towards the hierarchical system of the hospital, and the methods of care they have been trained in, is hardly surprising, but it is also one of the many barriers to change. It means that very often changes are proposed and implemented from above or from outside, and are thus resisted or felt as threatening by the nurses on the ward.

Increasingly, however, some nurses are looking for ways in which to change their roles within the hospital setting, and enlarge their roles outside.[22] The idea of the nurse as a 'social educator' or 'behaviour therapist' is increasingly gaining ground as a positive reaction to the criticism of hospitals. 'The nurse is being seen more and more as a creative homemaker who uses the social environment to produce change, instead of being a receiver or a custodian.'[23] The nurse's role in rehabilitation, behaviour modification, and social training is increasingly advocated by nurses themselves, and facilitated by the many courses that are now offered to them. What is striking is that the new roles envisaged for nurses are so firmly tied to the possibility of producing major changes in the behaviour of their charges. Behaviour modification, and other methods of training, have allowed nurses to define a new role for themselves *within* the existing hospital structure. This is a role that incorporates the current educational optimism about mentally handicapped people, but one which does not fundamentally question whether or not mentally handicapped people should be patients in hospital, looked after by nurses. Nor does it question the hierarchical nature of the hospital as a place to live or work in.

THE QUESTION OF SIZE

Size is another important question on which many of the arguments about hospital or other forms of care devolve. However, size is a very relative matter. After a 1,000-bed hospital the new 100–200-bed 'community' hospitals, with living units for eight to twelve people, can seem small. But they can seem enormous when compared to a 24-bed local authority hostel. And this in turn is much larger than a family, a small group home, or shared flat, even when subdivided into smaller units. Size is important from several different points of view – organization, specialist provision, developmental criteria, and local access.

One of the arguments used for hospitals is the 'comprehensive' one – that only where large numbers of handicapped people are grouped together can a sufficiently wide range of professional skills and specialist services be provided. This argument reflects the tendency for all state services to be reorganized into larger and larger units, with more remote control, for larger rather than smaller schools and hospitals to be built. It would be a more convincing argument if the quality of services in our present large hospitals was of a high standard – but many mentally handicapped people in hospital never receive these much vaunted specialist services. Furthermore, such services can be provided on a decentralized basis, and in several places this has been put into practice. In Melrose, for example, severely handicapped people are placed in local eight-bed units, rather than in the large hospital, and professionals from the hospital visit these units. The professionals are centralized, but the patients are not. And in the well-known Wessex hostels, residents have at least as much contact with professionals as they did in hospital.

In a comparative study of different kinds of residential care, Tyne found that larger-sized units severely restricted residents' opportunities for any kind of self-determination, either because of the degree of inflexible centralized organization, or because of the sheer number of other residents.[24] Lack of privacy, intrusions from other residents, competitiveness, the cumulative destructive effect of numerous handicaps, disruptive behaviour – all these problems were much worse in the larger living units.

Tyne found that small size was important in allowing flexible care, modifiable to each individual's needs, and giving residents some degree of choice in their daily lives. However, small size alone was not enough to ensure a better quality of life. In a few of the hostels, life was nearly as barren as in some hospital wards – the rules were inflexible, the staff authoritarian and the residents were isolated from outside contacts. Other people arguing for hostel care as against hospitals have tended to stress the developmental advantages of small living units. There is now overwhelming evidence that moving children from large wards into smaller living units produces great improvements in their behaviour. This has been shown both within and outside hospitals. The findings of the Wessex teams on their experimental hostels confirm this, for more severely handicapped people as well.[25] This latter finding is important because of the increasing trend in favour of hostel care for the least handicapped only.

The other aspect of the size question is that large residential units are inevitably not local ones. Residents have to be collected over a wide area, and this makes it extremely hard for contact between them and their families to be sustained, let alone for them to have a daily relationship. This factor alone exacerbates the 'put away' element of any kind of non-family care. The demand for local and therefore small residential facilities is one that parents overwhelmingly make. To remove mentally handicapped people from the easy access of their families and friends is not only a cause of profound distress in itself, but also a waste of one of the most important resources we do have – the people who care for their well-being, who want to continue to relate to them in some way, but need support in doing so.

These discussions of size tend to avoid the most challenging question of all – why do we assume that, whatever the nature of the living unit, mentally handicapped people should live with each other at all? There is no evidence that this is what they want, and every indication that they find living with other people who are incontinent or disruptive or very withdrawn as distressing as anyone else does. Until we really criticize the assumption that it is right for mentally handicapped people to live with each other, we are in danger of continuing to ghettoize them, however 'civilized' the new homes or hostels turn out to be. Most people do not live with people who have similar problems or disabilities as themselves, and do not on the whole show any desire to. It is possible that some (or indeed many) mentally handicapped people would prefer to live with each other – but at the moment they do not have any real choice in the matter. It serves other people's needs that they should live together, but not necessarily theirs.

This is not to imply that other people *ought* to want to live more closely with mentally handicapped people. The fact is that many people do, either from necessity or choice, and many more would want to if it was made possible. The success of a few pilot schemes that exist, where non-handicapped and handicapped people share a house together, with the former being paid for the support they give, show what a vast untapped potential there is for such an arrangement, despite pessimistic predictions that such schemes would not work.[26]

THE NEEDS OF THE STAFF

The arguments about the future of mental handicap hospitals often leave out any consideration of the needs of the staff themselves – any consideration, that is, apart from money, status and qualifications. The staff are in direct, daily, and sustained contact with mentally handicapped people, yet seldom is any serious thought given to what they need in order to do their work well and satisfyingly to themselves. This is a fundamental omission. Human resources are as important as financial, material, and technological ones. No amount of new buildings or new training programmes will produce the changes we desire if the people involved in these changes are not given adequate consideration and support themselves.

Several of the inquiries into hospitals have concluded that inefficient management and bad communication between staff were to blame for the unsatisfactory conditions and events. The solutions proposed were often purely administrative: different management structures, more joint or co-ordinating committees. Many of these solutions are simply experienced by ward staff as more 'red tape'. What they avoid is the fundamental political problem of working in highly centralized and hierarchical organizations. Streamlined management from above will not solve these problems. Many studies, both of hospitals and hostels, have now shown that autonomy for staff at living-unit level is vital for creating an individually orientated pattern of care for the residents and more satisfying work for the staff.[27]

In his comparative study of different living units, Tyne found that the degree of staff control over daily domestic tasks and social life, and over the allocation of resources (for example, food, cash, clothing) was an important factor in contributing to a more flexible life for the residents. In most hospitals this autonomy over everyday life was completely missing. Many staff in both wards and hostels were not sufficiently involved in planning, nor in discussions and decisions about the residents in their charge. The extensive survey on which the Jay report is based corroborated these findings: staff in both hospitals and hostels were more likely to be dissatisfied with their work where they lacked any influence over decisions taken about residents in their charge (for example, about transfers, admissions, training programmes), and where there was very little professional discussion involving them, about the aims of their work, or the progress of residents.

This lack of any real participation or power can make staff feel that they themselves don't matter to others; their sense of being disregarded then becomes disregard for their own work and for the people they are meant to look after.

Inadequate external support and guidance is another way in which staff in wards and hostels often feel undervalued. One of the nursing organizations refers to inadequate medical back-up within hospitals, and there are frequent complaints of how the various professionals – psychologists, speech therapists, etc. – are simply not interested, especially not in the more severely handicapped people.[28] Tyne found that in hostels professional support and advice, as opposed to administrative control and interference, were often missing. Discussion and advice were especially needed about the progress of individual residents, the goals to be set and implemented, how to deal with disturbing behaviour.

The way untrained nursing assistants are treated brings out the disregard in which their job is held, especially when it is remembered that they often form the majority of the staff in direct contact with the patients. In many hospitals they are commonly put straight on to the wards without any guidelines about what to do or expect, and with no kind of support for any difficulties they might encounter. They are simply expected to get on with the job, fit in with the routine, and there is very little helpful discussion about what goes on in the ward or about the individual patients, let alone the staff's own feelings or problems in the situation. The potential resources of people already working in the situation are simply suppressed and wasted. Creating a forum for discussion in each ward or hostel, where the life of the unit can be thought about honestly and openly, where staff can learn from and get support from each other and from the residents, would encourage everyone to value the importance of their work. These would have to be very different from the snappy case conference, or the usual ward meetings, where what the doctor or the nursing officer says automatically assumes greatest importance, and where no one reveals their own feelings of weakness or inadequacy.

Looking after mentally handicapped people involves creating and sustaining human relationships, not running an institution smoothly, or producing an acceptable product. That this even needs to be said shows how far we are from recognizing this as a central feature of the job, or of paying adequate attention to the emotional needs this creates in the staff. Part of what makes the work so hard is that neither the emotionally demanding nor the emotionally rewarding aspects of it are sufficiently recognized – and this goes for the staff themselves as well as people outside. Staff are exposed day by day to people whom society has rejected as worthless or too much trouble, yet they are also enmeshed in an ideology of 'caring'. Nurses work in an institution and a profession that does not recognize that they too might find their charges boring, disgusting, frightening, frustrating, but which tacitly, by its whole structure, sanctions unfeeling attitudes and impersonal methods of care. Making these negative feelings public, sharing them with other staff, would be a great step forward in recognizing the genuine difficulties of the job, accepting what it is taboo for nurses to feel, and finding ways to get support from others and make the work easier. Equally, making explicit the satisfactions of the job – the attachments formed, the progress made, the moments of humour and affection – would lead to a greater collective appreciation of the life of the living unit, and of the mentally handicapped people themselves.

In all the various plans for the greater normalization of mentally handicapped people's lives there is a notable absence of any attention to the emotional demands that this will create on the staff involved.[29] This omission is a recipe for failure. The Jay report, for example, whilst cursorily acknowledging the demanding nature of the job, simply paints a glowing picture of the paragons who will staff the various forms of more integrated homes. They will be people

... who are able to be themselves and who can allow their residents to be themselves; who are willing to accept their role as a very open one to be developed as the circumstances demand; whose warmth of care has few conditions attached to it; and who are able to care for people who are dependent without falling into the trap of kindly control. The staff will also need a belief in the capacity of all mentally handicapped people to move forward and a sense of their own contribution to the process.[30]

The report never once asks how people are to maintain such exemplary attitudes in the face of daily contact with people whose progress may be miniscule and whose dependency is very great. The question, 'Who cares for the carers?' is unasked and unanswered. We have seen in this book that it is often the staff who are in closest daily contact with the mentally handicapped who most have a need to distance and differentiate themselves from them, to see them as abnormal and unlike themselves. We have to come to grips with the personal needs and fears involved in this as well as the institutional and professional pressures that militate in the same direction. If we do not, we are in danger of planning for a future that will not be realized, and for a failure that will once again be blamed on the supposed incapacity of mentally handicapped people to 'move forward'.

DESPAIR AND THE DESIRE FOR CHANGE

Attitudes and feelings towards mentally handicapped people come from many sources. The social evaluation of mentally handicapped people as useless and abnormal creeps into the personal emotions we have about them, even though the reality of daily contact can be very different. There is no denying that at a personal and material level it is very much harder to be the parent of a mentally handicapped child than a non-handicapped one. Infancy lasts for much longer, but in a large and often incompetent body, each step that a normal child takes with hardly any effort has to be painstakingly learned with endless encouragement and repetition, more stimulation has to be provided and often less is received in return. But these very real demands hardly seem to account for the sense of disaster and despair that overtakes so many parents. Teaching and looking after mentally handicapped people require unusual patience, persistence and empathy, but this hardly explains the exaggerated admiration (superficial, as it often turns out) that outsiders express for anyone doing such jobs.

Why is slowness of development in a child, or dependency and inability in an adult, *so* hard for other people to accept? We find the behaviour of a three-year-old child acceptable (for the most part) but not the same behaviour in a 20-year-old. Playfulness that makes us delight in a child turns us to despair in an adult. Lack of muscular control that is normal in a two-year-old is horrifying in someone much older. For some the answer lies in an instinctive repulsion or turning away from the biologically abnormal, an answer which, likening us to animals, fails to take into account the deep effects of our culture, the massive disregard in which anyone who cannot be independent – economically, socially, and personally – is held. It is very hard to love or value someone who fails by a myriad of standards and norms, who does not conform or excel in any way. Many people in contact with mentally handicapped people – parents or staff – have a very deep need that they should change in some way, make some progress, become a little more acceptable. The depth of this need aroused by mentally handicapped people is seldom recognized. What we more often see is the despair and resignation that so little change is perceptible. The hope of possible change is often the only way of dealing with the pain of an unacceptable reality. The hope is often illusory because it is based on an unsatisfiable need – the need for someone not to be mentally handicapped at all, to change out of all recognition, to become normal.

The hopes that *could* be fulfilled are often not realized because we do not provide the right conditions – material and human – for an atmosphere of growth and development. It requires a very great amount of clarity, support and encouragement to maintain a positive environment for mentally handicapped people. Every step forward seems miniscule in relation to the standards of normality; long periods of time go by without much evidence of change. A supportive culture is needed to maintain a sense of positive development, and because this is so often missing, the experience of staff working with mentally handicapped people is often one of hopelessness and failure. It is easier to give up an unreachable goal than to continually fail to achieve it.

The new ideologies of normalization and behaviour modification make very great demands on the staff who have to implement them; they are often working towards a degree of successful integration into society which is in the short term unrealizable. This creates an unreal vacillation between hope and resignation, at both a personal and a social level. To say that false hopes are often generated by the enthusiasm for new technologies or new living arrangements is not to deny for one moment that as positive an environment as possible should be created for mentally handicapped people. It is simply to point out that we do them a disservice if we hold out unreachable goals, expectations that are contradicted by their social reality, and at the same time fail to recognize what unconscious needs of our own we are attempting to satisfy in the process. We have to be able to deal with the frustration of our own needs without, as usually happens, hurting mentally handicapped people with our sense of their failure.

We have seen in the field of mental handicap how much the spirit of reform, both past and present, is tied to the promise that mentally handicapped people can be improved – through changing become more acceptable. Again and again the path to greater acceptance is seen as through some kind of normality. It is no accident that the people who most have a philosophy of accepting mentally handicapped people as they are, are those who try to provide them with a refuge from the world rather than a path back to it. This philosophy of acceptance and appreciation is most espoused by the various religious, spiritual and alternative communities. Many of these communities have developed imaginative and intensive methods of education. It is not an attitude of resignation; the people in them are often looking for something different for themselves from many of the values that so condemn mentally handicapped people. They are not, as are most people, trying to live and work within most of the normal institutions of society.

From their writings they seem to have a strong appreciation of what mentally handicapped people can give to others. Such an appreciation is entirely missing from any of the professional writings of those who staff the hospitals – the doctors, nurses, psychologists, or administrators. Thus the founder of L'Arche communities writes:

Handicapped people, particularly those who are less able, are frequently endowed with qualities of heart which serve to remind so-called normal people that their own hearts are closed. Their simplicity frequently serves to reveal our own duplicity, untruthfulness, and hypocrisy. Their acceptance of their own situation and their humility frequently reveals our pride and our refusal to accept others as they are. So often so-called normal people have interior barriers that prevent them from relating with others in a simple way. All of us have deep needs to love and be loved. All of us are in the conflict of our own fear of death and of our own poverty. We so quickly pretend that we are more clever, more intelligent, and more powerful than we actually are. So often we flee reality by throwing ourselves into activity, culture, the struggle for power and prestige. We lose contact with our deep inner-selves. Handicapped people do not always have these barriers. In their poverty they are more simple and loving and thus they reveal to us the poverty of our riches.[31]

A similar kind of inspiration and appreciation is found in the practice and writings of those who follow Steiner. Weihs, one of the founders of Camphill village community, writes of the mongol child:

His love is not the love which is born of pain and consciousness; it is in a sense original love, love that is entirely innocent and unburdened by intellectuality. It is almost as if 'his eyes were yet not opened', as if the aura of human existence before the Fall from Paradise were still about him . . . [This love] is both his charm and attraction as well as his frailty and undoing, for it renders him nearly incapable of maintaining himself in our present day life and society . . . [And further] it can dawn on one that he is, perhaps, a kind of messenger come to remind his fellows that, in all their technical advancement in the pursuit of original causes, and in all their power to change their environment, they also have a mission to change themselves . . . One does not see only the pathology of his condition. In him one meets a new brother.[32]

These writings are much more than an invitation to take pity on the suffering; they are also a challenge to see what mentally handicapped people reveal about ourselves and the kind of society we live in. It is not just fanciful romanticization to claim that mentally handicapped people can be an inspiration to others, an indictment of the inhuman values of the rest of the world, a reminder of the buried and more vulnerable parts of ourselves. These perceptions are of decisive importance in allowing us to value them, in finding some common humanity. It is not intended here to draw any very direct comparisons between these religious communities and state institutions, because, impressive as the former often are, they usually depend on the total commitment and wageless labour of all the people in them. The most pertinent question is whether this kind of appreciation can be found and sustained outside of a religious or mystical context, in places that are not set up as an intended refuge from the world.

Frank in his diary reveals his appreciation of mentally handicapped people when he says:

I ended up hating the job, but respecting, even loving, the lads. The warmth and affection was always apparent if you gave it room to move. They don't hold back, no rigid socialization for them, no tempering of feeling and emotion. Showed whatever it was they felt – hatred, friendship, love.

Frank's appreciation is essentially a matter of emotional openness, something that can be encouraged or repressed.

Many people in the state institutions are attracted to working with mentally handicapped people from some kind of moral conviction: a desire to help, sympathy with the oppressed, guilt at their own advantages; and from some perception that all is not right with the world.[33] Often the work seems to offer some kind of meaning and satisfaction that is not offered by working in a factory or office. The professional and hierarchical world of the hospital does very little to encourage the ideas and enthusiasm that motivate many of its staff initially, and it often makes life very difficult for staff who do persist with their original perceptions.

If we are to ensure a better life for mentally handicapped people, we have to ensure that the people working and living with them are also in an environment where they can maintain their emotional openness and where they can recognize and respond to emotional needs – their own as well as their charges'. Caring for dependent people may be an unequal relationship but is by no means a one-way one. These reciprocal aspects are usually buried under the ideology of professionalism that most 'people's jobs' carry: the definition of 'them' as sick, weak and abnormal, and 'us' as competent, strong and normal. The staff of our institutions would be doing both themselves and mentally handicapped people a great service if they could begin to see themselves as part of the problem and not just as part of the solution. To do this, they, and we, the society that put them there in the first place, need to listen and respond to mentally handicapped people themselves.

Notes

Chapter 1. Definitions of Difference

1. In 1976 (the latest year for which there are statistics available), there were 48,773 patients resident in mental handicap hospitals, a rate of 105/100,000 population. Of these 37,703 had been there for more than five years. Source: DHSS, In-patient statistics from the *Mental Health Enquiry for England, 1976* (HMSO, 1979).

2. Roughly one-fifth of all handicap hospitals have 1,500–2,000 beds, and another fifth have 1,000–1,500, and nearly one-quarter have 500–1,000. Source: *Mental Health Statistics* (Mind publication, 1977).

3. From *Listen*, written by A. Shearer for Campaign for the Mentally Handicapped (1973). This is an account of a weekend conference for mentally handicapped people, held to encourage the free exchange of ideas and opinions between themselves and others.

4. ibid.

5. From R. Edgerton, *The Cloak of Competence* (University of California Press, 1971), a study of ex-patients living outside hospital in California.

6. From 'Residents speak out', in R. Kugel and A. Shearer (eds.), *Changing Patterns of Residential Services for the Mentally Retarded* (President's Committee for the Mentally Retarded, Washington, 1976).

7. E. Seguin, *Traitement moral, hygiène et éducation des idiots et des autres enfants arrières* (Baillière Tindall, 1846).

8. E. Seguin, *New Facts and Remarks Concerning Idiocy* (W. Wood & Co., 1870).

9. *Listen*, as note 3.

10. *Royal Commission on the National Health Service*, Cmnd. 7615 (HMSO, 1979).

11. The incidence of Down's syndrome is usually estimated at around 1 in 600 of all births, forming roughly 10% of all cases of mental handicap.

12. A full account of the medical and pathological categories of mental handicap can be found in books such as: L. Penrose, *The Biology of Mental Defect* (Sidgwick & Jackson, 1964), or L. Crome and J. Stern, *The Pathology of Mental Retardation* (J. & A. Churchill, 1967).

13. This is the estimate of the National Society for Mentally Handicapped Children (NSMHC). Other authors make statements to the effect that the majority of cases are undiagnosed, e.g. B. Kirman, in A. D. B. and A. M. Clarke (eds.), *Mental Deficiency: The Changing Outlook* (Methuen, 1974), without giving actual proportions.

14. In these two cases knowledge of the underlying biochemical disorder led to the development of corrective treatments, to be instigated from birth onwards. In the case of Down's syndrome, although the nature of the chromosomal disorder is well described, the cause of it is still unknown. Phenylketonuria is an interesting example of how a truly genetic (inherited) disorder is susceptible to environmental correction.

15. It has been estimated that in the UK at least 1,000 cases of *severe* mental handicap alone could be prevented each year by the full application of current knowledge, for example, immunization of pregnant mothers against intra-uterine infection, improved antenatal care, special care for low birth weight babies, wider screening for older mothers. Source: *Mental Handicap: Ways Forward* (Office of Health Economics, 1978).

16. *Lancet* (2 February 1974).

17. K. Holt and R. Huntley, 'Mental subnormality: medical train-

ing in the United Kingdom', *British Journal of Medical Education*, 7 (1973).

18. General Nursing Council evidence to Jay Committee, *Nursing Times*, 72, 16 (1976).

19. Source: DHSS, *Health Services Costing Returns, 1975/6* (HMSO, 1977). The cost per in-patient per day was £8.96 in handicap hospitals, £10.11 in psychiatric hospitals, and between £20.37 and £31.14 in general and acute hospitals. The cost of catering per in-patient per day was £00.91 in handicap hospitals, £00.95 in psychiatric hospitals, between £1.26 and £1.54 in general and acute hospitals, and £1.85 in maternity hospitals.

20. A. Tyne, *Who's Consulted?*, Enquiry Paper No. 8 (CMH, 1979), estimates that the number of medical staff – consultants and other doctors – is equivalent to $4\frac{1}{2}$ hours of patient time *per year*. There are only 0.84 medical staff per 100 patients altogether. Source: as note 1.

21. I. Leck, W. Gordon, T. McKeown, 'Medical and social needs of patients in hospitals for the mentally subnormal', *British Journal of Preventative and Social Medicine*, 21 (1967). Also, DHSS, *Better Services for the Mentally Handicapped*, Cmnd. 4683 (HMSO, 1971).

22. J. Tizard, *Community Services for the Mentally Handicapped* (Oxford University Press, 1964).

23. S. Hewitt, 'The need for long-term care', in *Occasional Papers*, 2, 3 & 4 (Institute for Research into Mental Retardation, 1972).

24. M. Bayley, *Mental Handicap and Community Care* (Routledge & Kegan Paul, 1973).

25. R. Edgerton, 'Mental retardation in non-Western societies', in H. Haywood (ed.), *Social-cultural Aspects of Mental Retardation* (Appleton-Century-Crofts, Inc., New York, 1970).

26. E. Reed and S. Reed, *Mental Retardation: A Family Study* (W. B. Saunders, Eastbourne, 1965).

27. See, for example, G. Lee and G. Katz, *Sexual Rights of the Retarded* (NSMHC, 1974).

28. DES, *The Education of Children in Hospitals for the Mentally Handicapped* (HMSO, 1979), shows that in a few hospitals some children received no education at various times, that a substantial proportion receive mainly on- rather than off-ward education, and that school hours are often extremely short.

29. See: B. Coard, *How the West Indian Child is Made Educationally Subnormal by the British School System* (Caribbean Education & Community Workers' Association, 1971), and J. Mercer, *Labelling the Mentally Retarded* (University of California Press, 1973). The latter is an extensive study of the influence of ethnic and socio-economic factors on the process of being classified as retarded. Such conflict between family and school is not inevitable: in Russia and China, for example, there is much more homogeneity between the values and attitudes transmitted by family and school, and such homogeneity is actively encouraged.

30. In Russia and China a different morality of achievement is inculcated, with different resulting pressures on the individual. In Russia, according to U. Bronfenbrenner, *Two Worlds of Childhood* (Pocket Books, New York, 1973), competition between whole classes or teams tends to be emphasized. In China where social cohesiveness and mutual support are regarded very highly, it is frequently emphasized how weaker pupils will be helped by stronger ones, and how the teacher will do everything to encourage rather than stigmatize a slower child. Once again it is the performance of the whole class rather than of particular individuals which is important. See N. Robinson, 'Mild mental retardation – Does it exist in the People's Republic of China?', *Mental Retardation*, 16 (1978).

31. *No Longer a Child*, Enquiry Paper No. 6 (CMH, 1977), describes some of the conditions and experiences of work in an adult training centre.

32. *Working Out* (CMH, 1975), is a report of a conference involving mentally handicapped people, who describe their experiences and difficulties in finding and keeping ordinary jobs. R. Edgerton, *The Cloak of Competence* (University of California Press, 1971), also provides a wealth of first-hand experience about work relationships.

33. P. Wildblood, in *Employment Opportunities for Mentally Handicapped People* (Proceedings of conference organized by Birmingham AEUW and CHCs, 1977), emphasizes the advantages of such workers, as does a recent Employment Services Agency leaflet, quoted in *Peace News* (8 April 1977).

34. G. Callaghan, *Employing the Mentally Handicapped* (Lincs. Community Health Council, 1976).

35. H. Braverman, *Labor and Monopoly Capital – The Degradation of Work in the Twentieth Century* (Monthly Review Press, New York, 1975). Braverman describes in great detail how both factory and office work have become deskilled and increasingly automated, and how the emphasis in selecting workers has been increasingly on discipline, loyalty, reliability etc., rather than on skills as such. The growing use of robots in many productive processes is a recent continuation of this trend, advertised, as are mentally handicapped people, as being of no trouble to the employer and not even needing tea breaks or holidays.

36. R. Edgerton, as note 5, provides the only detailed account of mental handicap in a whole range of societies. He maintains that one of the crucial factors in determining how well handicapped people are treated, and the degree of stigma attached to them, is whether or not there are special roles, usually religious ones, available for handicapped people to play.

37. For example, K. Jones, in *Opening the Door* (Routledge & Kegan Paul, 1975), found that nearly two-thirds of the nursing staff in her survey thought that the conditions of the hospital were as good as they could be with 'the type of patient' concerned.

38. From *Listen*, as note 3.

39. B. Ballinger, 'The viewpoint of the mentally subnormal patient', *British Journal of Psychiatry* (March 1973).

40. R. Edgerton, as note 5.

41. *Listen*, as note 3.

42. As L. Dexter maintains in 'A social theory of mental deficiency', *American Journal of Mental Deficiency*, 62 (1958).

Chapter 3. Care or Control?

1. It is striking that many of the inquiries and reports of recent years have occurred as a result of complaints and investigations by outsiders or by the media. Nurses who have tried to protest or criticize from inside have often been met with threats about their career prospects, or jobs (see Ch. 6, p. 117). So far, management and doctors have never broken ranks.

2. There is a large literature, mostly philosophical, on objectification. An extremely helpful discussion of the main features of objectifying relationships, and their historical and material basis is to be found in B. Fine, 'Sartre's critique of objectification and the case of the Panopticon', *Economy and Society*, Vol. 6, No. 4 (1977).

3. A. Shearer, *Listen* (CMH, 1973).

4. The staffing figures per 100 patients are as follows:

	1966	1974	1977	
Nursing staff	23.1	41.3	51.3	(of whom 22.3 were qualified)
Ward orderlies and domestics	3.5	9.8	12.1	

Source: DHSS, In-patient statistics from the *Mental Health Enquiry for England, 1976* (HMSO, 1979).

These figures show that over a ten-year period, staffing ratios have improved. What is not clear, however, is how this gets translated into actual staffing on the ward: length of shifts and overtime working have apparently decreased over the same period, reducing the effective staffing ratios (no figures available). Even with these apparent improvements it is not unknown for patients to die simply as a result of staffing shortages. For example, at St Lawrence's Hospital, Caterham, a child choked to death purely because there were not enough nursing staff available to feed him and supervise all the others (*Guardian*, 23 May and 25 May 1979). The hospital subsequently suspended all admissions until the staffing situation improved. Most hospitals operate with a large proportion of their posts unfilled, resulting in periodic acute crises.

5. A. Alaszewski, 'Suggestions for the reorganisation of nurse training and improvement of patient care in a hospital for the mentally handicapped', *Journal of Advanced Nursing*, 2 (1977).

6. This was what the chairman of the hospital training programme told the nursing staff in Frank's hospital.

7. From C. Hallas, W. Fraser and R. MacGillivray, *The Care and Training of the Mentally Handicapped* (John Wright & Sons Ltd, Bristol, 1974), a textbook for nurses.

8. DHSS, *Better Services for the Mentally Handicapped*, Government White Paper, Cmnd. 4683 (HMSO, 1971).

9. A. Alaszewski, 'Mental handicap and social policy: A case study of a care organisation', Ph.D. dissertation (University of Cambridge, 1979). This describes the classification categories of both the institution and the nurses, and the effects of these on patient care, at the Ida Darwin Hospital, Fulborn.

10. From M. Oswin, *Children in Long-stay Hospitals* (Spastics International Medical Publications, 1978), a study of the lives of multiply handicapped children in eight different hospitals.

11. A letter from a consultant to the head of nursing services, quoted in *Report of the Committee of Inquiry into South Ockendon Hospital* (HMSO, 1974).

12. P. Hughes, 'Survey of medication in a subnormality hospital', *British Journal of Mental Subnormality*, Vol. 23, No. 45 (1977).

13. A. Shearer, *Listen* (CMH, 1973).

14. E. Goffman, *Asylums* (Penguin, 1961). Most of Goffman's insights about total institutions apply to subnormality hospitals, although he does not explicitly consider them.

15. For illustrations of this, see P. Morris, *Put Away* (Routledge & Kegan Paul, 1969) and R. King, N. Raynes, and J. Tizard, *Patterns of Residential Care* (Routledge & Kegan Paul, 1971).

16. Much of the information on ward organization is taken from K. Jones (and others), *Opening the Door* (Routledge & Kegan Paul,

1975), a survey of several different institutions and an attempt to assess the impact of changing policy; and from A. Tyne, 'Nursing work and the care of the mentally handicapped', MA thesis (University of Essex, 1974) – a detailed study of one ward, and of nurses' perceptions of their work.

17. K. Jones, op. cit.

18. A. Alaszewski, as note 5.

19. R. King, N. Raynes and J. Tizard, op. cit., show how the much greater degree of autonomy and flexibility possible with less hierarchical systems, and with smaller units, leads to superior child-care, even within large hospitals.

20. K. Jones, op. cit., in a series of interviews with staff.

21. P. Morris, op. cit.

22. A. Tyne, op. cit.

23. M. Oswin, op. cit., has some examples of how staff provided expressly to play with the children rapidly became absorbed in the on-going domestic activity of the ward.

24. For example, K. Jones, op. cit.; A. Tyne, op. cit.

25. A. Alaszewski, as note 9.

26. K. Jones, op. cit.

27. A. Alaszewski, as note 9.

28. A. Tyne, op. cit.

29. A. Tierney, 'Toilet training', *Nursing Times*, 69, 51–2 (1973), provides a detailed account of a toilet training programme which not only resulted in greatly improved continence for the majority of patients involved, but also an overall improvement in their general level of functioning.

30. Evidence given at the Normansfield Hospital Inquiry, quoted in the *Guardian* (1 November 1977).

31. M. Oswin, op. cit.

32. A. Shearer, op. cit.

33. K. Jones, op. cit.

Chapter 4. The Outside World

1. P. Morris, *Put Away* (Routledge & Kegan Paul, 1969) and K. Jones, *Opening the Door* (Routledge & Kegan Paul, 1975).

2. K. Jones, op. cit.

3. M. Oswin, *Children in Long-stay Hospitals* (Spastics International Medical Publications, 1978).

4. *Mind Out*, No. 4 (1973), reports a meeting of parents where such experiences at Meanwood Park Hospital, Leeds, were discussed.

5. For example, see 'Involving the parents', *Nursing Times*, 69, 11 (1973).

6. J. Jacobs, 'Improving communications between health service professionals and parents of handicapped children: a case study', *British Journal of Mental Subnormality*, Vol. 23, No. 45 (1977).

7. For example, E. Cooper and R. Henderson (eds.), *Something Wrong?* (Arrow, 1975).

8. J. Gibson and T. French, *Nursing the Mentally Retarded* (Faber & Faber, 1974).

9. N. W. Hart, 'Frequently expressed feelings and reactions of parents towards their retarded children', in N. Bernstein (ed.), *Diminished People* (J. & A. Churchill, 1970). Some parents in this study felt that their child was a special message from God, a blessing in disguise, sent to test their faith. In S. Hewitt's study, referred to in Ch. 1, note 23, most parents simply felt that they had done the best they could to keep their child at home, and that hospitalization was eventually caused by the difficulties of the child's behaviour combined with the lack of supporting domiciliary services and the absence of any less drastic alternatives.

10. *Report of the Committee of Inquiry into South Ockendon Hospital* (HMSO, 1974).

11. A. Tyne, 'Nursing work and the care of the mentally handicapped', MA thesis (University of Essex, 1974).

12. K. Jones, op. cit. In her questionnaire study she found that 35% of the ward staff interviewed thought that little could be done to help low-grade patients to improve and 40% thought that therapy could achieve little with them.

13. M. Oswin, op. cit.

14. A. Alaszewski, 'Mental handicap and social policy: a case study of a care organisation', Ph.D. dissertation (University of Cambridge, 1979).

15. See *Group Homes: Special Report* (Cardiff University Social Services, 1976). This describes a small mixed hostel where students and ex-patients from Ely Hospital live together. Initially the scheme met with great pessimism from the hospital staff, particularly the consultant who predicted (wrongly) that residents would have to return to hospital within three months. It was also found that relatives visited residents more often in the hostel than the hospital (see description in *Kith and Kids* by M. and D. Collins (Souvenir Press, 1976).

16. E. Goffman, *Stigma: Notes on the Management of Spoiled Identity* (Penguin, 1970). Once again, apart from some footnotes, Goffman does not pay explicit attention to the situation that mentally handicapped people find themselves in. However, R. Edgerton, in *The Cloak of Competence* (University of California Press, 1971), extends Goffman's analysis to show how many mentally handicapped people engage in the tactics of 'passing' and 'denial' to appear as normal as possible, both to themselves and others. Edgerton emphasizes how the global nature of mental handicap, in affecting all aspects of a person's being, makes such tactics unlikely to succeed, but nonetheless necessary to a sense of self-esteem.

Chapter 5. The Historical Background

1. L. Kanner, *A History of the Care and Study of the Mentally Retarded* (C. C. Thomas, Illinois, 1964), presents useful information, especially about Europe. However, much of the book takes the form of a purely chronological list of events, the significance of which is not always evaluated. It reads a bit like official

history, with little sense of social process, of why events took place, or what related developments there were in society generally. Thus Kanner has to resort to unsatisfactory notions such as 'suddenly interest flared up' as explanations.

2. D. Rothman, *The Discovery of the Asylum* (Little, Brown & Co., Boston, 1971), provides an analysis of the social forces leading to the widespread creation of all types of asylums in America, in the late eighteenth and early nineteenth century. A. Scull, *Museums of Madness: Social Organization of Insanity in 19th Century England* (Allen Lane, 1979), tries to relate the growth of asylums for the insane to the increasing 'commercialization of existence' that took place in England, and also analyses how the medical profession got complete control of these asylums despite having very little to offer in the way of treatment or cures. Neither author, however, discusses idiot asylums, despite the importance of the same historical factors, and the similar development of the asylums from reform to repression under medical domination. Mental handicap has never received the kind of historical analysis that Foucault, for example, has provided for madness.

3. M. Rosen, G. Clark and M. Kivitz (eds.), in *The History of Mental Retardation* (University Park Press, Baltimore, 1976), particularly stress the development of humanitarian ideas in the nineteenth century, seeing all history before then as 'apathy dating from antiquity', which, as this chapter shows, is an oversimplified view. Seeing ideas and beliefs as major determining forces makes it difficult to explain changes in such ideas. Baumeister, for example, in A. Baumeister and E. Butterfield (eds.), *Residential Facilities for the Mentally Retarded* (Aldine, Chicago, 1970), also seeing the nineteenth century as the 'age of professional altruism', has to attribute the subsequent change in the nature of institutions to the 'swing of the pendulum' – what pendulum and who set it swinging anyhow?

4. All the following quotations are taken from Paracelsus, *De Generatione Stultorum*, translated by P. Cranefield and W. Federn as 'The begetting of fools', *Bulletin of the History of Medicine*, 41 (1967), with an annotated discussion. Paracelsus's treatise was written around 1530 and published in 1567.

5. St Augustine, *Migne Patrologia Latina*.

6. A congenital condition is one which is present from and caused before birth, but which is not inherited, in the sense that the parents do not have or carry the same condition.

7. Grimm, quoted in C. Haffter, 'The changeling: history and psychodynamics of attitudes to handicapped children in European folklore', *Journal of the History of Behavioural Sciences*, 4 (1968).

8. ibid.

9. ibid.

10. ibid.

11. See P. Cranefield, 'The discovery of cretinism', *Bulletin of the History of Medicine*, 35 (1961).

12. J. Simler, quoted in P. Cranefield, as note 11.

13. Haller, a Swiss physician, in 1793, quoted in P. Cranefield, as note 11.

14. W. Coxe, *Annual Register* (1779); a traveller's account of Swiss cretins that excited much interest and speculation.

15. ibid.

16. Even now there is relatively very little ecological research into the prevalence of specific forms of mental handicap – research that could possibly reveal the presence of important toxic agents in the environment. And even when such agents are known (for example, lead and mercury poisoning), the caution of scientists in drawing conclusions from such findings and of governments in putting into practice relevant action, is in marked contrast to the readiness with which vague hereditary theories and policies of segregation and sterilization have been adopted.

17. See P. Cranefield, 'A seventeenth-century view of mental deficiency and schizophrenia – Thomas Willis on stupidity or foolishness', *Bulletin of the History of Medicine*, 35 (1961).

18. D. Defoe, 'A hospital for natural fools', in *An Essay upon Projects* (1697), excerpted in R. Hunter and I. Macalpine (eds.), *Three Hundred Years of Psychiatry* (Oxford University Press, 1963).

19. E. Seguin, *Traitement moral, hygiène et éducation des idiots, et des autres enfants arrières* (Baillière Tindall, 1846).

20. 'Idiot asylums', *Edinburgh Review*, Vol. 122 (1865).

21. Quoted in L. Kanner, op. cit.

22. Rev. E. Sidney, 'Teaching the idiot', a lecture given in 1854.

23. E. Seguin, *Idiocy and Its Treatment by the Physiological Method* (Kelley, New Jersey, 1866).

24. As note 20.

25. E. Seguin, as note 23.

26. E. Seguin, as note 19.

27. G. Shuttleworth, *Mentally Deficient Children: Their Treatment and Training* (H. K. Lewis, 1895), quoting a much earlier remark of Esquirol, a French physician who was one of Seguin's predecessors.

28. S. Howe, *The Causes of Idiocy* (Maclachlan & Stewart, 1848).

29. F. Bateman, *The Idiot: His Place in Creation and His Claims on Society* (Jarrold & Sons, Norwich, 1897). Bateman was a physician at the Eastern Counties Asylum, Colchester.

30. A report on Highgate Asylum in 1850, a few years after it was opened, as note 20.

31. Description of Earlswood Asylum, opened in 1855, quoted in 'Idiot asylums', as note 20.

32. Recommendation in P. Duncan and W. Millard, *A Manual for the Classification, Training and Education of the Feeble-minded, Imbecile and Idiotic* (Longmans, 1866).

33. E. Seguin, as note 23.

34. As note 20.

35. E. Seguin, *New Facts and Remarks Concerning Idiocy* (W. Wood & Co., 1870).

36. As note 20.

37. See P. Duncan and W. Millard, op. cit., for detailed descriptions of all these matters.

38. As note 20.

39. *68th Report of the Commissioners in Lunacy* (1914). Cited in A. Alaszewski, *Mental Handicap: A Liberal Humanitarian Reform?*, Occasional Papers (Institute for Health Studies, Hull University, 1977).

40. K. Jones, *A History of the Mental Health Services* (Routledge & Kegan Paul, 1972).

41. I am indebted to D. Rothman's, *The Discovery of the Asylum* (Little, Brown & Co., Boston, 1971), for this point, which he illustrates in detail in relation to other kinds of asylum.

42. A. Scull, op. cit., gives a very detailed account of this.

43. See note 3.

44. Rothman, op. cit.

45. A. Scull, op. cit.

46. For example, P. Duncan and W. Millard, op. cit., who describe the gentleness, obedience, comfort and moral influence to be found in the asylum, as compared to the harshness and neglect of working-class family life, where idiots are often kept locked up or else abandoned. J. Langdon-Down, *The Education and Training of the Feeble in Mind* (H. K. Lewis, 1876), argues that proper education can only be carried out in institutions where every detail of life can be ordered.

47. S. Howe, op. cit.

48. E. Seguin, as note 23.

49. E. Seguin, as note 35.

50. W. Ireland, *On Idiocy and Imbecility* (J. & A. Churchill, 1877).

51. G. Shuttleworth, op. cit.

52. F. Bateman, op. cit.

53. A. Tredgold, *Mental Deficiency – Amentia* (Baillière Tindall, 1908).

54. G. Shuttleworth and W. Potts, *Mentally Deficient Children* (H. K. Lewis, 1904).

55. J. Langdon-Down, lecture at London Hospital, 1866, quoted in L. Kanner, op. cit.

56. G. Shuttleworth, as note 27.

57. From M. Barr and E. Maloney, *Types of Mental Defectives* (P. Blakiston, 1921).

58. A. Tredgold, op. cit.

59. *Report of the Royal Commission on the Care and Control of the Feeble Minded*, Chairman: Lord Radnor (HMSO, 1908).

60. Quoted in A. Alaszewski, as note 39, who provides a very useful analysis of this period.

61. *Report of the Mental Deficiency Committee, Part 111 – The Adult Defective* (HMSO, 1929).

62. Study by L. Penrose, cited in *The Biology of Mental Defect* (Sidgwick & Jackson, 1964).

63. *17th Annual Report of the Board of Control* (1930), quoted in A. Alaszewski, op. cit., note 39.

64. C. Burt, *The Subnormal Mind* (Oxford University Press, 1977).

65. *Report of the Departmental Committee on Sterilization*, Chairman: Lord Brock (HMSO, 1934).

66. D. Stafford-Clark, *Psychiatry Today* (Penguin, 1961). Similarly defamatory statements are to be found in D. Stafford-Clark and A. Smith, *Psychiatry for Students*, 5th edition (Allen & Unwin, 1978), and have been the target of widespread protests to the publishers who have promised to rework the whole presentation of mentally handicapped people in the next edition of this widely used textbook. See CMH newsletters, Nos. 14 and 15, for details of the book and campaign against it.

67. Source: Board of Control's Annual Reports, 1930–39.

68. A. Binet and T. Simon, *Mentally Defective Children* (Edward Arnold, 1914).

69. C. Burt, op. cit.

70. See J. Ryan, 'IQ – the illusion of objectivity', in K. Richardson and D. Spears (eds.), *Race, Culture and Intelligence* (Penguin,

1972), for a critique of the whole idea of 'innate' intelligence as something measurable by IQ tests.

71. *68th Report of the Commissioners on Lunacy* (1914).

72. See P. Cranefield, note 17.

73. For example, S. Howe, op. cit.

74. For an account and a critique of this approach to mentally handicapped people, see J. Ryan, 'Scientific research and individual variation', in A. D. B. Clarke and A. M. Clarke (eds.), *Mental Retardation and Behavioural Research* (Churchill Livingstone, 1973); also by J. Ryan 'The production and management of stupidity: the involvement of medicine and psychology', in D. Robinson and M. Wadsworth (eds.), *Studies in Everyday Medical Life* (Martin Robertson, Oxford, 1977). It is only recently that a less narrow and more developmental approach to intelligence has become common, particularly with the greater popularity of Piagetian ideas.

75. A more detailed account of this fundamental categorization is to be found in J. Ryan, second reference, note 74. The conclusion of A. D. B. Clarke and A. M. Clarke (eds.), in *Mental Deficiency: The Changing Outlook* (Methuen, 1974), is that less than one-third of the numbers of mental defectives predicted by IQ test statistics, extrapolated downwards, are actually ascertained. Their conclusion is that most of the remaining number are functioning happily in the community rather than that there is something amiss with the basis of the prediction.

76. A. Jensen, 'A theory of primary and secondary familial mental retardation', in N. R. Ellis (ed.), *International Review of Research in Mental Retardation*, Vol. 4 (1970).

77. See L. Kamin, *The Science and Politics of IQ* (Halsted Press, New York, 1974), for a critique of Burt's original twin data, and the subsequent use of it by Jensen and others.

78. For a review of this, see J. Ryan, 'Classification and behaviour in mental subnormality', in D. Primrose (ed.), *Proceedings of the 2nd Congress of the International Association for the Scientific Study of Mental Deficiency* (1970).

79. Mental Health Act 1959.

80. M. Mannoni, *The Backward Child and His Mother* (Pantheon, New York, 1972), provides a psychoanalytic study of the effect of a handicapped child on the mother–child relationship.

81. By P. Nichols (Faber & Faber, 1967).

Chapter 6. Old Ideologies for New

1. A. Shearer, 'The news media', in R. Kugel and A. Shearer (eds.), *Changing Patterns of Residential Services for the Mentally Handicapped* (President's committee for the Mentally Retarded, Washington, 1976), gives an illuminating account of these events in which she was an important participant.

2. R. Crossman, *The Diaries of a Cabinet Minister: Vol. III 1968–1970* (Hamish Hamilton, 1977).

3. *Report of the Committee of Inquiry into Mental Handicap Nursing and Care*, Chairman: Peggy Jay, Cmnd. 7468 (HMSO, 1979).

4. This summary of the figures is taken largely from *Plans and Provisions for Mentally Handicapped People*, Enquiry Paper No. 4 (CMH, 1976), and *Residential Provision for Adults Who are Mentally Handicapped*, Enquiry Paper No. 5 (CMH, 1976). In the former, the fear is expressed that, as of 1973, the net provision, hospital and otherwise, of all residential provision had actually fallen, due to the relatively slow growth of the local authority residential sector (from 5,221 places in 1970 to 10,158 in 1977, according to the Jay report).

5. In 1976 the number of children under 16 in mental handicap hospitals was 4,263 compared to 6,648 in 1970. Source: *Helping Mentally Handicapped People in Hospital* (National Development Group, 1978). However in 1977, the then Minister of Health admitted that the number of local authority residential places for mentally handicapped children was the same as in 1969. D. Ennals, quoted in CMH Newsletter, No. 11 (1977/8).

6. Source: as note 4, and *Whose Priorities?* (Radical Statistics Health Group, 1976).

7. *Report of the Committee of Inquiry into Normansfield Hospital* (HMSO, 1978).

8. *Services for the Mentally Handicapped in Hampshire* (National Development Group, 1978).

9. Letter from a charge nurse to David Ennals, Minister of Health and Social Security, published in *Mind Out*, No. 21 (1977).

10. *Helping Mentally Handicapped People in Hospital* (National Development Group, 1978).

11. M. Oswin, *Children in Long-stay Hospitals* (Spastics International Medical Publications, 1978).

12. A. Tyne, *Looking at Life in a Hospital, Hostel, Home or Unit* (CMH, 1978).

13. See for example, E. Cooper and R. Henderson (eds.), *Something Wrong?* (1975), and M. and D. Collins, *Kith and Kids* (Souvenir Press, 1976), both vivid accounts of the despair of parents having to cope with not only their handicapped children, but also the ignorance, condescension and unhelpfulness of various 'professionals'. *Kith and Kids* is remarkable for the extensive self-help schemes it initiated.

14. Field End House, Islington. See CMH Newsletter, No. 14 (1978) for description.

15. DHSS, *Better Services for the Mentally Handicapped*, Cmnd. 4683 (HMSO, 1971).

16. A. D. B. Clarke and A. M. Clarke (eds.), *Mental Deficiency: The Changing Outlook* (Methuen, 1974).

17. See for example, N. O'Connor, 'Psychology and intelligence', in M. Shepherd and D. Davies (eds.), *Studies in Psychiatry* (Oxford University Press, 1968).

18. A. D. B. Clarke and A. M. Clarke, as note 16.

19. Thus many experiments involve comparisons between groups of handicapped children living in institutions and groups of normal children living at home. The precision with which these experiments are carried out, and with which statistical analyses of the result are performed, makes an absurd contrast with the way in

which the subjects' social experience and present living conditions are completely ignored and uncontrolled. This methodology characterizes a very large number of psychological experiments, including those by some of the leading researchers in the field, such as N. O'Connor and B. Hermelin, *Speech and Thought in Severe Subnormality* (Pergamon Press, Oxford, 1963). For a more thorough critique see J. Ryan, 'The production and management of stupidity: the involvement of psychology and medicine', in M. Wadsworth and D. Robinson (eds.), *Studies in Everyday Medical Life* (Martin Robertson, Oxford, 1977).

20. A. D. B. Clarke and A. M. Clarke, as note 16.

21. A. Jensen, 'A theory of primary and secondary familial mental retardation', in N. R. Ellis (ed.), *International Review of Research in Mental Retardation*, Vol. 4 (1970).

22. A. D. B. Clarke and A. M. Clarke, as note 16. Also for research on reaction times specifically: A. A. Baumeister and G. Kellas, 'Reaction time and mental retardation', in N. R. Ellis (ed.), *International Review of Research in Mental Retardation*, Vol. 3 (1969).

23. K. Marx, *The German Ideology* (Lawrence & Wishart, 1848).

24. For an understanding of IQ as primarily a rate measure, see J. Ryan, 'IQ – The illusion of objectivity', in K. Richardson and D. Spears (eds.), *Race, Culture and Intelligence* (Penguin, 1972).

25. A. D. B. Clarke and A. M. Clarke, as note 16. Also J. Ryan, 'The silence of stupidity', in J. Morton (ed.), *Psycholinguistic Series*, No. 1 (1977), for an account of the interaction processes between parents and handicapped children.

26. P. Duncan and W. Millard, *A Manual for the Classification, Training and Education of the Feeble-minded, Imbecile and Idiotic* (Longmans, 1866).

27. The extreme vulnerability of multiply handicapped children to their barren environment is painfully shown in M. Oswin's study cited in note 11 above. Their fragile attempts to play with objects or make contact with other children were frequently thwarted rather than encouraged by the unthinking routine of the hospital.

28. See: 'Handicapped by preconceptions', *Nursing Mirror*, 141, 21 (1975).

29. J. Elliott in 'Perspectives on the Briggs report', *Mental Handicap Papers*, No. 4 (King's Fund Centre, 1975).

30. For example, A. Tierney, 'Toilet Training', *Nursing Times*, 69, 51–2 (1973).

31. M. Oswin, op. cit., describes a lengthy programme in which some multiply handicapped children were taught to feed themselves by a psychologist. In the ward, however, they were seldom encouraged to use these skills because they were so slow that the nurses preferred to continue feeding them. This illustrates one of the funda mental pressures that handicapped people are up against – *time* – and its meaning in our society – *productivity*.

32. See for example, A. Murray, 'Implementing a behaviour modification programme', *Nursing Times*, 73, 5 (1977).

33. Quoted in M. Oswin, op. cit.

34. B. Nirje, 'The normalization principle', in R. Kugel and A. Shearer (eds.), *Changing Patterns of Residential Services for the Mentally Retarded* (President's Committee for the Mentally Retarded, Washington, 1976).

35. *The Rights of the Mentally Handicapped* (CMH, 1973).

36. A. Tyne, in *Looking at Life in a Hospital, Hostel, Home or Unit* (CMH, 1978), provides the first significant attempt to assess the quality of life of mentally handicapped people in various settings by specifying what he thinks their needs are. These he categorizes under three main headings: daily needs (food, warmth, sleep); needs for personal identity (privacy, relationships, activities); and needs for development and growth. Some of the items included are ordinary and common to most people, some are special to mentally handicapped people some of the time (for example, provisions for incontinence, disability or behaviour problems, protection from the consequences of other people's disabilities, special health care).

37. H. Gunzburg, 'The hospital as a normalizing training environment', in H. Gunzburg (ed.), *Advances in the Care of the Mentally Handicapped* (Baillière Tindall, 1973).

38. K. Day, 'Care of the mentally handicapped', in A. Baker (ed.), *Comprehensive Psychiatric Care* (Blackwell Scientific Publications, 1976).

39. As note 3.

40. B. Nirje, in R. Kugel and A. Shearer (eds.), as note 34.

41. N. Bank-Mikkelson, Denmark, in R. Kugel and A. Shearer (eds.), as note 34.

42. *Who are These People Anyway?* (Mind/CMH pamphlet, 1977).

43. K. Day, in A. Baker (ed.), op. cit.

44. R. Conley, *The Economics of Mental Retardation* (John Hopkins University Press, Baltimore, 1973).

45. D. Ennals, in Foreword to *Helping Mentally Handicapped People in Hospital* (National Development Group, 1978).

Chapter 7. Which Way is Forward?

1. From Royal College of Psychiatrists' Memorandum, 'The way ahead in mental handicap', *British Journal of Psychiatry* (September, 1977), quoted in A. Tyne, *Who's Consulted?*, Enquiry Paper No. 8 (CMH, 1979), an investigation into the roles and attitudes of doctors in mental handicap hospitals.

2. ibid.

3. W. Heaton-Ward, *Left Behind – A Study of Mental Handicap* (Macdonald & Evans, Plymouth, 1977).

4. G. Harris (consultant, St Lawrence's Hospital, Caterham) at Mental Handicap Conference, King's Fund Centre, London, June, 1978.

5. J. Michelson and P. Tinsley, 'A thesis on the future role of the subnormality hospital and the care pattern for the mentally handicapped' (unpublished paper, 1971).

6. Some of these frustrations were voiced at the Leavesden Group Conference, 'National Day on Peggy Jay' in 1976.

7. W. Heaton-Ward, op. cit.

8. *Report of the Committee of Inquiry into South Ockendon Hospital* (HMSO, 1974).

9. W. Heaton-Ward, op. cit.

10. D. Spencer, letter in *British Medical Journal*, 1, 44 (1978).

11. RCP's Memorandum, *British Journal of Psychiatry* (August, 1976).

12. RCP's Memorandum, *British Journal of Psychiatry* (October, 1976).

13. A. Shapiro, *Lancet*, 11 (1969), p. 957.

14. R. Crossman, *The Diaries of a Cabinet Minister: Vol. III 1968–1970* (Hamish Hamilton, 1977).

15. A. Tyne, as note 1.

16. Articles on the Hospital Action Group, in *Therapy*, 4,19 (1978), and *Nursing Mirror*, 146, 13 (1978).

17. M. Oswin, *Children in Long-stay Hospitals* (Spastics International Medical Publications, 1978).

18. Article on Wessex mixed-ability hostels in *Mind Out*, No. 28 (1978).

19. 'Still no way, Mrs Jay', Leader in *Nursing Mirror*, 148, 10 (1979), refuting the proposals of the Jay report.

20. For example, P. Reynolds, 'Nurses are the experts', *New Psychiatry*, 2 (1975).

21. R. Gladstone, in 'Patients who never complain', *Nursing Mirror*, 148, 23 (1979), describes the Jay proposals for a social work rather than nursing training as 'like telling a man who has enlisted in the Guards that he was to be trained by the Boy Scouts'. Clearly the patient who complained that being in hospital was like being in the army (ch. 3 p. 65), was not so far wrong.

22. As at the Leavesden Conference, note 6.

23. J. Elliott, 'Perspectives on the Briggs report', *Mental Handicap Papers*, No. 4 (King's Fund Centre, 1975).

24. A. Tyne, *Looking at Life in a Hospital, Hostel, Home or Unit* (CMH, 1978).

25. As note 18.

26. For example, *Group Homes: Special Report* (Cardiff University Social Services, 1976), where students lived with handicapped people discharged from Ely Hospital. The consultant predicted the ex-patients would return in 3 months but in fact the scheme has been very successful. A few other similar schemes have been started.

27. For example, R. King, N. Raynes and J. Tizard, *Patterns of Residential Care* (Routledge & Kegan Paul, 1971); A. Tyne, as note 24.

28. General Nursing Council evidence to the Jay Committee, *Nursing Times*, 72, 16 (1976).

29. The one exception to this is an article by A. Shearer, 'The Caring Staff', in R. Kugel and A. Shearer (eds.), *Changing Patterns of Residential Services for the Mentally Retarded* (President's Committee for the Mentally Retarded, Washington, 1976).

30. *Report of the Committee of Inquiry into Mental Handicap Nursing and Care*, Chairman: Peggy Jay, Cmnd. 7468 (HMSO, 1979).

31. Jean Vanier, quoted by A. Shearer, 'L'Arche', in R. Kugel and A. Shearer (eds.), as note 29.

32. T. Weihs, *Children in Need of Special Care* (Souvenir Press, 1977). See also K. Konig in C. Pietzner (ed.), *Aspects of Curative Education* (Aberdeen University Press, 1966).

33. In the survey on which the Jay report is based nearly half of all the nursing staff, and 57% of the local authority hostel staff said they took up this work because of their interest in 'caring for people', 23% of the nursing staff said it was because they specifically wanted to work as nurses in a clinical role.